P9-BJE-558

TANTRA

THE ART OF CONSCIOUS LOVING

TANTRA

THE ART OF CONSCIOUS LOVING

BY CHARLES AND CAROLINE MUIR

Mercury House, Incorporated
San Francisco

Copyright ©1989 by Charles and Caroline Muir

Design by Sharon Smith
Illustrations by Debbie Drechsler

Published in the United States by
Mercury House
San Francisco, California

Distributed to the trade by
Consortium Book Sales & Distribution, Inc.
St. Paul, Minnesota

All rights reserved, including, without limitation, the right of the publisher to sell
directly to end users of this and other Mercury House books. No part of this book
may be reproduced in any form or by any electronic or mechanical means, including information storage and retrieval systems, without permission in writing from
the publisher, except by a reviewer who may quote brief passages in a review.

Mercury House and colophon are registered trademarks
of Mercury House, Incorporated

Manufactured in the United States of America

Library of Congress Cataloging-in-Publication Data
Muir, Charles.
    Tantra: the art of conscious loving / by Charles and Caroline Muir.
      p.   cm.
    ISBN 0-916515-55-9
    ISBN 0-916515-86-9 (pbk.)
    1. Sex—Miscellanea. 2. Magic. 3. Tantrism. I. Muir, Caroline. II. Title.
BF1623.S4M83   1989
131—dc19   88-7854
                                                                        CIP

20 19 18 17 16 15

*This book is dedicated to
the Spirit of the Mother*

CONTENTS

PART I
TANTRA FOR COUPLES

ONE   HAPPILY EVER AFTER   3

A look at love in our times, the promises that personal independence and growth offer, the disappointment when the honeymoon is over. What happens to passion? What do men want from women? What do women want from men? Are their differences resolvable?

TWO   THE TANTRIC WAY   15

An examination of Tantra's age-old system of loving; the science of the "subtle body"; the sexual/spiritual connection; the importance of focusing the mind, of becoming a conscious practitioner.

THREE   TANTRIC HARMONY   29

The role of harmony in partnership; balancing yin and yang; the nurturing meditation; breathing techniques to restore balance; the couple as a team.

FOUR   TANTRIC COMMUNICATION   37

Learning the conscious language of love; the master archer; three steps to restoring harmony; gifts of love.

ACKNOWLEDGMENTS

The authors acknowledge the following people for their help in making this book: J. Michael Kanouff, Doris Ober, Alev Lytle Croutier and the team at Mercury House, Marbie Ingalls, Anurag, and Sapan.

Caroline expresses her deep and everlasting gratitude for the men and women who have shared with her the ways of Love: Sonny, Rick, Ron, Gina, Tucker, Ronnie, Singh Kaur, and especially her beloved grandfather, Nank. She adds special thanks "for the union with my greatest love, Charles, who is my teacher and mate for the rest of this life."

Charles sends thanks and blessings to all the teachers on his path who have taught him about Love, especially Bobbi, Michaeline, Mary, Jeannie, Abigail, Jwala, Emily, Diane, Sherry, Jill, Diana, Mercury, Alana, Whitestar, Yaz, and Singh Kaur. He adds, "Special thanks, love, and adoration to my current teachers: Pauline Siggia Muir, who has taught me since birth about love, dedication, and service; my son and guru, Orion; the Tara; and especially my beloved wife, Caroline, who is the fruit and seed of my path."

Special credit and thanks to our many students who over the years have helped us learn more about ourselves, more about others, and more about the art of loving.

INTRODUCTION

The word *Tantra* refers specifically to a series of esoteric Hindu books that describe certain sexual rituals, disciplines, and meditations. These ancient Indian books, over two thousand years old, were written in the form of a dialogue between the Hindu god Shiva, who is "the penetrating power of focused energy," and his consort, Shakti, who represents the female creative force and is sometimes called "the Power of Tantra." Ancient Tantra is a spiritual system in which sexual love is a sacrament. We are not teachers of ancient tantric traditions and rituals, but we have developed a system based on tantric philosophical concepts and techniques that we have found applicable in our life and in the lives of our students. It is a system that can elevate a couple's relationship to the level of art. We refer to it as the Art of Conscious Loving.

Unfortunately, and contrary to what we would like to believe, we are not born naturally good at sex or at relationships. Few of us have benefited from a formal education in sexuality or sexual love. Even though we are children of the sexual revolution, we are still largely conditioned by belief systems that may have instilled in us guilt or fear or insecurity or shame. Such negative imprints, although they may reside quietly in the subconscious and cause only minor or occasional disturbances, rarely allow us to journey into the spiritual potential of sexual love. Tantra can help us do just that because a spiritual goal is as important to the tantric couple as their love.

Tantra is a school of many courses in which there are many levels of study and an unlimited degree of potential for spiritual gain, for sexual delight, and for worldly success. In our workshops and seminars we use techniques that we have developed from some of the ancient tantric lessons. These techniques are designed for the uninitiated, for the beginner. We share them with love and with deep respect for the potential for pleasure, for healing, and for spiritual growth they can provide.

It is one of the tenets of tantric philosophy that the discipline—the tantric lessons—is reborn age to age. We hope you will share our excitement over how extraordinarily well suited to our modern age and culture these ancient eastern lessons are. They are important tools for today's couples who are searching for a significantly different way of relating to each other, couples who want to sustain love and sexual passion for a lifetime together. We have seen men and women leave our seminars and workshops in a heightened state of awareness of themselves and of their love, and we have been gratified to learn from the many cards and letters we receive that this heightened awareness between them was not just an anomaly, not just a fleeting occurrence, but has become a permanent part of their relationship. Tantric sex does not promise instant results; it is not a "one-minute" technique for achieving sexual prowess. But for couples who want to enrich their relationship, it can release a particular kind of energy that can bring about harmony between them and increase their sexual pleasure and intimacy. In sum, tantric sex can create an extraordinary partnership.

We've arranged this book in two parts. The first is an initiation into Tantra, its goals, its philosophy of life, and the science on which its practice is based—how it works, in other words, and specifically how it works for the couple. The second part addresses sexual rituals, the yoga or "union" couples practice to achieve an ecstatic connection in loving.

Charles and Caroline Muir
Kahului, Hawaii

PART I

TANTRA FOR COUPLES

ONE

HAPPILY EVER AFTER

The wedding was celebrated in great splendor, and they lived happily to the end of their days.

"BRIAR ROSE," in *The Complete
Fairy Tales of the Brothers Grimm*

These days, not many of us believe in happily ever after. Statistics show that well over half the married couples in our culture divorce, and many of those who stick it out do so for reasons other than personal happiness—because it's such a hassle dividing everything, moving, having to start over—not to mention children and the emotional and financial aspects of splitting up. In this practical twentieth-century climate, it's hard to take happily ever after as much more than a metaphor in which "ever after" means "for a while."

Theoretically, this definition could allow a person to live happily ever after if he or she lived in consecutively happy-for-a-while relationships. These were fashionable to a degree in the sixties and seventies, but became first questionable and then dangerous in the eighties as the AIDS epidemic was recognized and understood. But it is not just fear of AIDS that is changing contemporary relationships. In our seminars we meet men and women whose desire for partnership stems from a feeling that there is something important to be gained from a significant relationship. And it seems to be more than a desire to "settle down." Couples today are looking for a commitment from each other, but a special kind of commitment—one that contains a spiritual as well as a physical element and emotional and psychological aspects as well as material ones.

This is a fairly new phenomenon, and in this regard we may indeed have entered a New Age. For one thing, the concept of "marrying for love" is relatively new, popular only in the past 150 years or so. Before that, material and political considerations took precedence over any kind of attraction, emotional, physical, or intellectual, and most matches were arranged among families. Consider also how the social-sexual aspects of relationships have evolved over the past hundred years in our western culture, beginning with a period of Victorian values and attitudes that loosened its laces at the turn of the last century but didn't toss away its stays until the 1920s and 1930s. In the forties, war romanticized relationships at the same time that it tore them apart, and the fifties inherited the results of that war; people entered the era of the atom bomb with a determination to make the nuclear family work. Then came the sexual revolution of the sixties, which spawned the women's movement of the seventies and its demand for social and sexual equality. And so into the eighties, the post-sexual-revolution era, a time of personal movement and personal freedom that the media dubbed the "me" generation. Now, as we approach the turning of another century, men and women seem to want to face life together. This may be the start of the "we" generation, a generation that desires an end to the battle of the sexes and the beginning of a new form of relationship in which partners work together as a team to satisfy needs, uplift one another, and journey together toward personal growth and sexual and spiritual fulfillment.

PROMISES

The past few decades made us some promises of sexual sophistication, personal independence, and prosperity. For a large number of men and women today, many of these promises have been fulfilled. We enter into relationships richer than any previous generation. We are richer in knowing more about the world because the media communicate information to us daily, and travel is within the means and personal experience of most of us. We are richer because we know more about ourselves—in fact, we are a culture fascinated with itself. We draw elaborate astrological charts and attempt to read the future in the stars. We analyze the past and present in therapies ancient and avant-garde. We take care of our bodies, we exercise and eat well, we stop smoking. We look to improve. We practice positive affirmations. We visualize bright futures.

Being so blessed, so evolved, why are we less successful than previous generations in making relationships last? Why do we have such a hard time relating to one another for an extended period of time? As we enter an era in which long-term personal partnerships are increasingly important, it seems critical to address these questions and to answer them.

IF WE'RE SO SMART, HOW COME WE'RE NOT IN LOVE?

There's love, and then there's Love. There's passionate love, and then there's love after passion or without passion. The latter has been known, in fact, to be quite cozy and satisfying in many ways; but love without passion may also deteriorate into as pale a version of the original as benign tolerance, and there is the risk that it may die completely or turn into resentment or disrespect, or worse.

It is not dispassionate love that we want to discuss. We want to focus on love that is full of passion and heat, love that makes your blood fairly pulse inside you; love that is all the nourishment you need. This is the love that overcomes all obstacles, dissolves time, obsesses you, possesses you, and radiates from you so that people comment on your "glow," and are drawn to you as if by a magnet. This is love that expresses itself sexually as a wonder, the best ever. It is so for both of you—you can't get enough of one another.

Love is not necessarily blind, as Shakespeare claimed, but it is surely an altered state. Physicians tell us that biochemically, love shares a lot of the same exhilarating effects that amphetamines produce. We know that the immune system can be strengthened by it;

5

that white blood cells perform better; and that the production of endorphins increases. We feel terrific!

So what happens? What causes passion to close its doors after such a promising opening to such good reviews?

Part of the answer can be found if we consider passion as a kind of energy that depends on other energy for its survival. When we are in the early passionate stages of a relationship, we expend a lot of energy trying to win one another, enchant, impress, and attract one another. We mentioned that passionate love overcomes obstacles. It is the *energy* required in that overcoming that is most significant. For example, when men and women decide to live together, they eliminate one of the biggest obstacles of all—physical separation—but they don't realize that they are removing something that has contributed to their passion. They need to find a way to compensate for the energy-hole their relationship experiences when they no longer need to overcome the obstacle of living separately. They have created an energy void, and passion suffers for it. The diminution of energy diminishes passion.

In the early stages of a love affair, passionate energy seems self-generating. The newly attracted couple is in a nearly constant state of arousal. They're charged. They're superconductors. And then, usually, the lovemaking falls off—quantitatively, anyway. It's less *urgent* once you've come to trust your relationship, come to rely on your partner, gotten to be "familiars." We *want* to trust one another and rely on one another—but why must we lose Love?

In fact, we don't have to lose anything. What usually happens is that the lessening of lovemaking means a lessening of energy in the relationship. When couples don't make that physical connection as often, the atmosphere changes. Love begins to stagnate and energy is directed elsewhere.

Men and women who are passionate about their work, or their art, or their politics are recognized for the energy they manufacture in order to pursue and maintain and advance the endeavor to which they are devoted. In the same way, men and women who are

6

passionate about their relationship must be committed to manufacturing the energy needed to sustain it. This is especially true in an era that offers so many opportunities and so much personal freedom. Many of us have several passions, and sometimes the amount of energy spent pursuing them exceeds the amount of energy they return. When this happens, we operate with a "passion deficit." We have to borrow energy from other sources to compensate. Ultimately, unless we rectify the deficit at its source, we will suffer serious losses. Too often one of these losses is passion. We meet many couples who are simply too busy or too tired to make love. Both work, they have children, they contribute time and energy to their community and to their church. They're concerned about self-improvement, so they devote several hours a week to their health and physical fitness. Many have aging parents to look after.

It is a fact that modern couples are on the go. They're exhausted by the end of the day, and sex is the last thing on their minds. The irony is that making love can provide both partners with more energy. The reality is that when a couple lessens their lovemaking they begin the not-so-slow process of starving their love. Love is nourished by the sexual energy a couple generates.

THE PASSIONATE PARTNERSHIP

A passionate partnership not only needs the nourishment sexual energy provides, it also needs maintenance. *Conscious* maintenance. We believe that as much care, thoughtfulness, and attention should be paid to a relationship as to a career, a family, or a cause. Unfortunately, this is not a popular concept. More popular, but less realistic, is the theory that love, having visited itself upon us, is here to stay; that a relationship, once established, will operate on automatic, will be self-sustaining, and will not interfere with the partners getting on with their individual lives. Furthermore, couples expect their relationship to augment and complement them professionally, creatively, socially, and economically. That's a lot to ask of coupledom; but in fact a loving relationship *can* provide nourishment in all areas of life. It *can* generate energy enough not only for itself but also for work, family, friends, hobbies. But this doesn't happen by magic. A relationship is like a garden. If it's not watered, weeded, pruned, fertilized—cared for—its yield suffers. If it's untended it goes to seed. One of the main reasons relationships deteriorate is that the partners neglect them.

Another reason is that partners don't communicate their needs to one another. Many people are too shy or too afraid to say what they need in order to feel loved, or whole, or just happy. Some people don't know the words, or they are afraid of having their needs rejected or of being thought less of for being needy, or they are ashamed of their needs. So they sometimes hold back what's in their hearts or on their minds, and when they finally do express themselves, having stewed too long in silence, the communication comes out a little too sharp, or too flat. We need to learn how to communicate with one another as lovers and as partners, and we need to find a different form of communication from the ones we use elsewhere in life. We'll discuss this subject more fully in Chapters Three and Four.

In addition to neglect and lack of communication, preconceptions about what the relationship *should* be can also cause problems. These preconceptions are often deep-rooted: they are based on what we observed of our parents' relationship while we were growing up; on how church, society, and the media promoted relationships then, and on what is acceptable now; and on our own experiences in relating to people—family, friends, lovers—and how these people have related to us. Our personal histories and past experiences are part of who we are, and so of course they have an influence on our partnerships. *But when we become a couple our new relationship should have no history, only a present and a potential future. Part of what we do in living the relationship, in fact, is to create a history for it together.*

Every couple is unfairly burdened by histories and experiences that insinuate themselves into the present. She mustn't forget that "men are liars and cheats," for example. He'd better remember that "women can't be trusted," that "they are likely to reject a man sexually or abandon him entirely on a whim, any time."

And yet we are drawn to one another. Men and women have the undeniable urge to merge. Whether coupling is symbolic of attaining union on a higher level, or whether the urge is purely biological, the desire to become one with our beloved is undeniable. And in our fervor, it is possible to mistake oneness for sameness. *In fact, we are not the same. In fact, it is the differences between a man and woman that can make their combination succeed.*

We don't mean irreconcilable differences, of course. Nor do we mean that men and women are different in every way. We share a lot, and we are naturally drawn to someone who is like ourselves in certain ways—someone with a similar sense of humor, for instance, or a common background, or a shared sense of right and wrong, or similar goals and dreams. The differences we are talking about are those basic ones that actually distinguish male from female—the differences in sexual nature. Attempting to satisfy a passionate relationship while denying these differences is almost always impossible. But when one understands the nature of the differences between the sexes, one can learn to capitalize on them, making them work to the advantage of both partners and to the advantage of the relationship. Because in fact the differences are complementary—what a man lacks, a woman has to spare, and vice versa. Learning how to make your differences an asset to the relationship—learning how those differences can fulfill the relationship instead of eroding or depleting it—is what this book is all about.

VIVE LA DIFFERENCE

Men and women today look for similar things in a relationship and they desire them to similar degrees: We want psychological security from one another; we want to be able to trust one another; we want to support one another, emotionally as much as economically;

we want to share similar experiences, to be playmates as well as responsible partners; we want to improve ourselves through our relationship and we hope that the relationship will improve with us; and truly, we want to love one another for a lifetime together.

The fact that a couple shares similar goals for their relationship bodes well for them because it signifies the couple's appreciation for their partnership as an entity in and of itself. It focuses them on *it* as separate from *us,* and this point of view is crucial to the health and well-being of the partnership.

However, while men and women may not be so different in what they want for themselves as a couple, we know from our seminars that they are very different when it comes to what they want—in fact, need—for themselves as sexual individuals in the relationship.

For example, we have found that most women use the word *intimacy* to describe what is most important to them sexually. Sexual intimacy (as expressed by the women we meet) is a special kind of closeness, a communication that is deeper than the couple can achieve physically, a sharing that goes beyond material partnership. This profound connection is described by many women as a spiritual connection, or as the feeling of having found one's "soulmate." Women relate it to the heart or the soul more than to the brain or the genitals, although when true sexual intimacy does occur, sexual passion is its by-product. This seems to be true in all areas, not just sex. When one becomes "intimate" with a subject or project, is immersed in it, "gets into it," one becomes passionate about it—excited, energized, turned on. It's the same with sexual intimacy—a woman is aroused, stirred deeply and physically.

But when intimacy is missing, when a woman doesn't make that special connection with her partner, she remains unsatisfied at a primal level because this need for intimacy is so deep. When intimacy is missing, it's hard for many women to feel passionate or to be satisfied, and the more deficient in intimacy a relationship becomes, the more dispassionate and dissatisfied the woman feels.

10

For most men, however, the word *intimacy* conveys something very different. Most twentieth-century western men are ecstatic when they hear a woman say she wants sexual intimacy—*needs* it. Because to them the words *sexual intimacy* mean intercourse. So if in the beginning of the relationship the woman seemed to be getting a satisfactory amount of sexual intimacy, measured by the amount of sexual passion the couple exchanged, and the man's not doing anything different in sex today except trying harder to get some, whose fault is it? What went wrong?

These are common questions for couples today, and they represent a serious misunderstanding of terms—a major failure in communication at the very cornerstone of the relationship. It's easy to project the resentment and anger, the frustration and hurt feelings, even the embarrassment, that are bound to occur between two people who haven't communicated their most basic needs to one another, who have misunderstood one another, who have been

11

operating on incorrect assumptions, perhaps for years. And it's easy to envision how their relationship will suffer.

Because the need for sexual intimacy is so basic to women, it must be defined by each woman for herself, and then she must communicate its personal meaning to her lover. This is not so easy to do. By nature and physically, women are sexual introverts; they *contain* their sexuality. Their sexual organs, their most sensitive places, are internal and protected. It's not difficult to understand how this might affect a woman's ability to speak out about her deepest sexual feelings, how protective she might feel about them. But a woman absolutely must be able to make her lover understand what intimacy means to her. When she does, her effort will be rewarded a thousandfold.

It's far less difficult for most men to communicate what they need for themselves as sexual beings, or to express what keeps them passionate. Man's sexual nature is fundamentally extroverted, and he projects obvious physical evidence of what turns him on. Quite simply, sex turns most men on. Sex makes them passionate. Men love sex—they love two bodies, naked, tangled together. Men are crazy about women who love sex. Intimacy may be nice, certainly psychological and emotional compatibility are important, but for the vast majority of the men we work with, sex is a barometer for the health of their relationships, and a healthy relationship is one with a goodly quantity of good sex. To oversimplify (there are many exceptions and gradations to these feelings), most women want a heartfelt or soulful experience in love, most men want a glandular one.

Occasionally this discrepancy becomes a weapon in a relationship headed for self-destruction—for instance, when a woman withholds sex from her partner to punish him (often because he's not sharing intimacy with her), or when a man won't give his woman the intimate connection she needs, won't cuddle with her, won't look deeply into her eyes and say he loves her (often because she never wants sex). This couple is on a self-perpetuating disaster course. The colder he is toward her, the less inclined to passion is she; the less inclined she is, the colder he gets. You can practically hear the seconds ticking down for this couple.

So what is the answer? We have different desires, men and women—they are physiological, basic to our male and female natures. They seem, if not opposite to one another, at least not conjunct. How can these differences be reconciled?

The solution we teach in our seminars and workshops is based in part on the tantric "lifestyle" that was designed centuries ago specifically for householders—that is, couples. The tantric texts are explicit on how the differences between the sexes can be used as a positive force in a partnership, how the proper combination of these differences can produce a near-alchemical reaction, an ether in which everything flourishes, in which the garden of your relationship bursts with color and new life and growth, and you and your beloved thrive.

TWO

THE TANTRIC WAY

The six regions of the body
The five states
They all have left and gone
Totally erased
And in the open
Void
I am left
Amazed…
The Unobtainable Bliss
Has engulfed me…

PATTINATTAR, A TAMIL TANTRICA,
in *The Poets of the Powers,* edited by Kamil V. Zvelebil

Although relics of tantric rituals date back nearly five millennia, the tantric texts began to appear within a few centuries of the beginning of the Christian era. There are said to be 108 original volumes in which the tantric system is defined and its practices enumerated, but there are numerous commentaries and essays, or "expansions," upon the first books, which are also known as Tantras (the word *Tantra* means expansion).

These ancient books offer their practitioners a complete way of living; they encompass physical and material realms, mental and psychological aspects, and spirituality. Although it has gained a reputation for being the "yoga of sex," Tantra's sexual element is only a part of its focus, a part of a means to an end. Tantra's goals are more exalted and broader in scope than simply accomplishing proficiency in love. The ultimate goal is Unity. Tantricas aspire to a spiritual connection or union, to experience the individual self as part of the Indivisible All. To help them attain Unity, they employ techniques of visualization and meditation and they practice ritual sexual union and a highly developed form of communication with a partner.

Although we interpret some of the ancient tantric teachings from an end-of-the-twentieth-century point of view, it is not our intention to replace tantric goals or methods with our own. Tantra was our inspiration as we developed a system to help provide contemporary partnerships with a great reservoir of regenerative energy that expresses itself sexually, physically, and creatively. Before we get into a "how to" discussion of this system, we will briefly introduce you to the paradigm, or larger-than-world-view on which tantric theory is based, and then to the science of it.

TANTRIC VIEW OF REALITY

To help us understand the tantric philosophy, we need to make a distinction between a higher plane of reality, a state of cosmic consciousness, which we will refer to as Reality with a capital R, and our microcosmic or worldly reality, which we will call reality with a lowercase r. In our lowercase reality, there exists a fundamental condition of duality that expresses itself as *masculine* and *feminine*. This is not an exclusively eastern concept; many cultures demonstrate a similar perception in their languages. The Romance languages, for example, designate objects and subjects by gender. Tantra, too, sees that everything in this reality contains masculine and feminine energies. But in that uppercase Reality, this duality does not exist. In the higher Reality one finds Unity. There is no masculine or feminine; there is only the One. Tantra's word for the One is *Shiva-Shakti*, the union of cosmic consciousness with creative energy, the force that moves creation, the perfect combination of masculine and feminine that produces the undifferentiated One.

Remember, the tantric goal is that condition of Unity or Oneness. In more contemporary terms, we might say that the goal is to achieve self-actualization, or personal integration, or simply whole-

16

ness. For Tantricas, the couple is the vehicle in which one crosses from reality to Reality.

TANTRIC SCIENCE

Early tantric sciences included mathematics, medicine, astronomy, and surprisingly sophisticated atomic, space-time, and sound wave theories, as well as alchemy, palmistry, and astrology. Tantra is credited with inventing the decimal, discovering zero in ancient India, and introducing the concept of *chakras,* or psychic energy centers, as part of human biology. (The word means "wheels" or "disks" of energy.)

Among the most beautiful of tantric artifacts and relics are the paintings and scrolled charts that illustrate these chakras in men and women. Chakras are organs of the energetic or *subtle body,* which is considered to be distinct and independent from the outward physical or *gross body.* Tantra recognizes five layers of the body, which are called *sheaths.* The outermost layer is the skin and bones. Next is the more subtle system of respiration; beyond that is the even more subtle system of cognition. Then comes discretion, and finally, most subtle of all, the chakra system, the body's intuitive or psychic energy system through which one may achieve physical ecstasy and spiritual unity.

There are seven major chakras in the subtle chakra system, each of which is both a generator and a reservoir of energy and psychic consciousness. The chakras are connected to one or more of the five sheaths by means of "subtle channels" called *nadis.* In this way the energy from each of the chakras nourishes the whole body. These channels are not unlike the meridians on which acupuncture is based, and they are also similar to our understanding of the body's neural connectors and circuitry.

THE SYSTEM OF THE SEVEN CHAKRAS

In tantric art, each of the seven major chakras is symbolized by a different lotus blossom to signify its particular nature. Each blos-

SEVENTH CHAKRA
Crown of head
Formless supreme
   light
Yantra: lotus flower
   with 1000 radiant
   petals
Mantra: OM (ends as
   ...MMM in the
   seventh chakra)

SIXTH CHAKRA
Between the eyebrows
Yantra: full moon color and shape
Mantra: OM (begins as OOO...
   in the sixth chakra)

FIFTH CHAKRA
Throat
Ether element
Yantra: white circle
   inside inverted
   triangle
Mantra: HAM

FOURTH CHAKRA
Heart
Air element
Yantra: six-pointed star
   inside circle
Mantra: YAM

THIRD CHAKRA
Behind the navel
Fire element
Yantra: inverted red
   triangle inside
   circle
Mantra: RAM

SECOND CHAKRA
Genital area
Water element
Yantra: moon-
   colored crescent
   inside circle
Mantra: VAM

FIRST CHAKRA
Base of spine
Earth element
Yantra: inverted red
   triangle inside
   yellow square
Mantra: LAM

Note: Each mantra is pronounced to rhyme with "mom" except OM, which rhymes with "home." The OM mantra begins as "OOO..." in the sixth chakra and ends as "...MMM" in the seventh chakra.

som is composed of its own combination of colors, petals, and symbolic designs. Each is understood to contain a positive or a negative charge, a numerical and an alphabetic value, a particular affinity with an element of nature (air, earth, water, etc.), with one of the several senses (taste, touch, smell, etc.), and with a particular tonal quality. This latter aspect suggests an analogy: Consider the chakras as the strings of a guitar. Each string vibrates at a different frequency and gives off a different note. Over time the strings may resonate sharp or flat, and they require tuning. When they are in tune, the sound the guitar produces is harmonious. Similarly, when the chakras are in tune, one achieves harmony.

Each chakra corresponds to a specific area of the body, and each is believed to generate a particular form of what we call "drive." The seven chakras align through the center of the body, with the spine as their axis. They begin at the base of the spine with the first or base chakra. According to the tantric books, the first chakra's drive is toward the material; its desire is to acquire and possess. Ironically, its bodily function deals with elimination. The second chakra is located in the region of the genitals, out of which is generated the sex drive. The third chakra, behind the navel, relates to power issues and influences the digestive system. The fourth chakra, which governs respiration, is near the heart, and is considered the energy source for intimate connection. The fifth chakra, at the throat, influences the glandular system and contains the drive to communicate as well as the spiritual drive. The sixth chakra exists between the eyebrows, where it generates intellect, and in the back part of the brain (the reticular formation), where it affects consciousness as well as the potential for inner vision. A "thousand-petaled lotus" represents the seventh chakra, which is located at the crown of the head inside the cranium and also in the area just above the head, in that realm we seek outside of ourselves. When this exterior portion of the seventh or crown chakra is emanating energy, we refer to it as a halo.

Although a western skeptic might raise an eyebrow over much

of the system we've just outlined, similar metaphorical values apply in our own perception of the human body. For example, we make an obvious association with the first chakra, located just above the anus, when we refer to "anal retentiveness," or when we say that a person who seems extremely possessive or obsessive is "tight-assed." And few would deny the powerful charge that occurs in the region called the second chakra when one is sexually aroused. This is the reproductive center—a *generator* of the most creative sort.

The third chakra controls digestion and affects the drive for power. We know it as the solar plexus, and we are certainly familiar with its energetic expression on a physical level. We call someone "gutsy" who demonstrates drive and forcefulness; we know that a "gut-level" feeling about something should be respected. This area is the site of ulcers in many modern-day westerners who are simply "driving" themselves too hard.

The fourth chakra, too, is easy to envision in contemporary terms. Eastern tradition ascribes to the heart rulership of compassionate instincts, of love and sympathy and intimate association; and western language echoes this ascription. We say "Have a heart!" when we ask for mercy or compassion; we talk about heartbreaks and heartthrobs and heartaches. We know what a heartwarming situation is, and that it is not measured by Fahrenheit or centigrade. We are often "led by our heart," when we think we should be directed by our head. And although we don't literally mean that our heart has us on a leash, we do mean that we are moved, directed, affected by some power or influence the heart has over us.

It's easy enough to accept that the fifth chakra, located in the throat, holds the equipment for communication and that the voice, a function of vibration, is an energetic expression. The fifth chakra's symbolic relationship to spirituality may be harder to fathom, but we do know that emotion expresses itself in this region. We get a "catch in the throat" when we are moved, for example, and we feel our "heart in our throat" in extreme situa-

20

tions. We can appreciate the throat's symbolic position as the connector of the body to the mind—the mind being the gateway to a spiritual union—if we remember that at the end of life, in the ultimate spiritual journey, a "death rattle" may occur in the throat. This is considered to be the sound of the soul departing the body on its way into the cosmic arena.

The sixth chakra, source of intellectual energy, cognition, and concentration, can be viewed as a metaphor for the brain and the brain's power or energy. Some people call the sixth chakra the "third eye," and ascribe to it powers of inner vision or insight.

Each chakra, then, represents a natural human desire—to possess, to copulate, to achieve, to love, to communicate, to understand, and finally to ascend, to exceed ourselves by touching God or the cosmic consciousness or a higher level of being, or whatever your words are for it. The tantric way uses these natural urges in men and women as the basis for establishing a continuously passionate loving relationship.

THE SEXUAL / SPIRITUAL CONNECTION

It is traditional in many cultures, even western cultures, to practice celibacy in the pursuit of spiritual life. This is true as well for the hundreds of schools of yoga that recognize sexual energy as a spiritual force, and aim to conserve that energy for the spiritual path. But celibacy as a spiritual motivator pretty much limits the quest for a raised form of consciousness to a cloistered community; and of course, if everyone followed this path, the number of people making a spiritual journey would quickly diminish and disappear.

Today many of us common folk aspire to spiritual growth. But we also desire to grow with a partner. Tantric yoga was the path couples chose thousands of years ago to satisfy this dilemma, since the tantric discipline allows men and women to have a mate, to enjoy sex, *and* to experience spiritual fulfillment, often simultaneously. How can this be? How can sexuality coexist with spirituality—the one base, the other sublime? For an answer we look inside,

21

to the Tantra's subtle body, and to its ascending energy centers, beginning with the most "base" and ending in the cosmic zone.

At the first chakra, coiled tightly like a spring at the base of the spine, resides what Tantra calls *kundalini shakti*. Its literal meaning is "coiled feminine energy," but it exists in men and women to the same degree, and could as well be called "creative energy," or "life energy," or "motivating energy," or the "energy of pure consciousness." This energy exists inside us as well as outside of us, which means that we contain within us that which we seek; spiritual connection, that higher Reality we strive for, need only be awakened from inside ourselves to be realized.

When the kundalini is aroused it begins to unwind, releasing its energy up through the body. It follows the spinal column to the second chakra, the third, the fourth, and higher. And as it goes, its near-electric charge imparts energy to and receives energy from the seven body centers, awakening dormant consciousness as it ascends, until it unites with the topmost chakra, and in so doing achieves its goal: Unity, spiritual ecstasy, called *ananda* in Sanskrit. Ananda is also known as *nirvana,* as *satori,* as enlightenment, as sainthood. The tantric texts assure us that it is within the grasp of each of us. In fact, the books call it our birthright.

Achieving the tantric goal of Unity, however, can take a lifetime of study and devotion, and it is not our purpose here, although envisioning the possibility of attaining such a goal and working toward it can enhance all aspects of life. In our seminars we encourage couples to remain aware of this ultimate tantric goal as they strive for Unity in their relationship. If your practice of the art of conscious loving leads you to desire more information about Tantra, we suggest you consult the bibliography at the back of the book as a starting point.

Before leaving this very brief discussion of the kundalini, we need to point out that this energy is released in varying degrees in each person. It may be stirred but not uncoiled; it may be aroused but not propelled with enough force to make its way all the way up through the body. Often it becomes stuck very close to home, in the second chakra, where it expresses itself sexually and then retracts to its original position and goes back to sleep. The forced and premature awakening of kundalini energy can be dangerous. The techniques for creating and releasing energy that we use in our seminars and share with you here are safe and very gentle. If at any time, however, you feel uncomfortable with any of them, we urge you not to do them. Wait for a time when you may be more receptive, or simply pass over them.

FOCUSING THE MIND

Tantric yoga is practiced in a serene, calm frame of mind, a condition that is often difficult to achieve in our high-tech, high-stake, fast-paced world. Tantra urges meditation, the conscious turning of the mind away from things of this world, in order to experience a deep inner peace.

To help us get to that state, Tantra offers several techniques. Concentration is one, and while it seems simple enough, it is not

23

easily achieved. To aid us in our efforts to concentrate, Tantra suggests a variety of meditations that directly affect the brain, quieting the intellectual, analytical left hemisphere and activating the experiential, intuitive right hemisphere. It is in the right hemisphere of the brain that "mystical" experiences transpire. (As a general rule, to the extent that a person is operating in the left side of the brain during lovemaking, he or she misses much of the ecstatic potential tantric sexual love offers.)

Another method to still the mind is a breathing technique called "cosmic intercourse." To practice this exercise, focus awareness on your spine beginning at the base chakra, and then bring that awareness up in a slow, deep-drawn inhalation, conscious of each energy center on the spinal axis, from base to crown. At the end of the inhalation, hold your breath for three to ten seconds, during which time you should try to actually feel the energetic air that fills the cranium at the crown of the head, the "Seat of Shiva." Now begin the exhalation, also a slow, deep breath, as you accompany that rarefied air back down through your body, visiting the same energy reservoirs in the opposite direction, maintaining awareness all the while. At the base chakra, hold your breath out

A YOGIC BREATH
CONSISTS OF 4 PARTS:

1. Slow inhalation.
2. Several seconds of
   held breath.
3. Slow exhalation.
4. A moment's holding of the
   breath out or pause
   before beginning the next
   inhalation.

for several seconds, and focus your mind on this reservoir or seat of kundalini energy. Then begin again. The rhythm is one of waves washing up a sandy shore and back, up and back, smoothing the beach, like a caress. Try it now; it will refresh and relax you. As you inhale, picture the air freshening each spinning wheel of energy inside you; as you exhale let your breath carry away all the day's exhaustion.

Breath control as a technique for establishing a meditative state is common to all yogic disciplines. In eastern traditions it is the breath that keeps the vital life-force circulating throughout the body. To control the breath is to increase life's essence. For tantric couples, breath control is one of the most important techniques for achieving the interpersonal harmony required to sustain and nurture the relationship.

Intermediate and advanced students of Tantra use two other powerful techniques to deepen their meditations and their physical and energetic connections. These are yantra and mantra techniques. *Yantras,* literally "tools," are symbolic or archetypal diagrams. There are 960 of them in total, all symbolic of various aspects of cosmology. Like a *mandala,* also a graphic representation of the cosmos, the yantra is considered a "power image"; its geometry, its spatial characteristics, its elements of dynamism are designed to appeal to the psyche and to cause a specific mental response—in this case, a focusing of the mind. Yantras send a geometric thought wave to the chakras that says, "Awaken! Purify! Activate!" In our workshops we use the seven yantras that correspond to the seven chakras described earlier (see page 18). Initiates begin by staring at the yantra diagrams, in ascending order. Once the designs have been learned their visualization, combined with a deep, palpable awareness of the corresponding chakra centers, is a very effective method for focusing the mind in meditation.

Bija mantra is another advanced technique for awakening, purifying, and activating the chakras. These mantras are the tonal equivalents of yantras, vibrational syllables that stimulate and resonate with the seven chakras to create a harmonic inner chord. Repeating these syllables as a chant acts like a tuning fork to bring the mind to peace and awaken the chakras' dormant energies. Most of us are familiar with the syllable *OM*, considered to be the "sound of the universe." Its associated chakras are the sixth and seventh. The mantras (all pronounced to rhyme with "mom" except the final "OM," which rhymes with "home") and their corresponding chakras are shown in the chart on page 18.

Mudras are also used by advanced students of Tantra in the ritualistic focusing of the mind. These are forms of nonverbal communication that use various hand and finger gestures and body postures to symbolize aspects of the higher Reality and to influence and redirect energy to parts of the body not usually empowered in this way, including the regions of the higher chakras.

Tantricas also practice *White Tantra* techniques as a form of meditation and to focus the mind. White Tantra is the grandfather of what we know as Hatha Yoga; it uses beneficial stretching techniques combined with breathing, concentration, and "feeling," to direct awareness and emotion to the physical body, which activates the chakra system. It is the breathing, concentration, and feeling aspects of White Tantra that separate it from most forms of Hatha Yoga.

We mention some of these more advanced techniques so that you will be aware of them and can learn more about them when you desire. They are not essential practices for *elementary* students of Tantra, but they grow in importance as you advance, and they will add variety and depth to your mind-focusing techniques.

There is another aspect to concentration and mind focusing in tantric yoga that is very important to the successful practice of the art of conscious loving because it allows us to shift the focus from the individual to the couple. In this way, couples can sustain concentration on their relationship as much as on one another. This is not as easy as it may sound. It takes effort to remain continually conscious, or focused, or attuned to one another and to the relationship. But this is a large part of tantric discipline, and it plays a very important role in our programs. To be considerate, in the most literal sense, of the other *and* the we *and* the I, to stay awake, is in fact the key to the passionate and evolutionary, perhaps *revolutionary*, relationship that Tantra offers.

THREE

TANTRIC HARMONY

And when Love speaks, the voice of all the gods
Make heaven drowsy with the harmony.

SHAKESPEARE, *Love's Labour's Lost,* act IV, scene iii

We touched briefly on the concept of polarity, or duality, in the last chapter. This concept is fundamental to tantric art, science, and ritual. It is the basis for the Tantricas' philosophy of life as it manifests on earth and in the beyond, and it is the operating principle, based quite literally on the attraction of opposites, in their special partnerships. In the case of the couple the principal opposites are male and female, but those designations mean much more in eastern parlance than a mere biological identification. Maleness is understood to hold certain properties, many of which are recognized in western ideology—positiveness and extroversion, for instance—but in addition the eastern perception of the male principle includes lightness and heat (the sun is a male symbol). The female principle, on the other hand, is dark and cool (the moon is a female symbol); it carries a negative energetic force, and it represents a receptive condition (which is introverted and intuitive as well as accommodating). Aspects that characterize maleness are referred to as *yang,* and those with female qualities are called *yin.*

The tantric goal is to achieve a state where opposites cease to exist, where yin and yang are in perfect balance and duality is eclipsed. On a spiritual level this condition is considered a state of bliss, of ecstasy, of Unity. On a worldly plane, the goal is the same— tantric partners want to fit together as neatly as yin and yang. They seek a perfect balance where their differences are complementary.

They aim for an ecstatic combination—the experience of bliss, love, and Unity—in their relationship.

Men and women are personifications of duality by their very masculine and feminine natures. If we think in terms of energy, as Tantricas do, we can understand how the combination of these opposite natures can create a potentially dangerous high-voltage situation, like putting two live wires together. A couple may create fission instead of fusion; or the intrusive energy of the world, with all its obligations and responsibilities, may cause interference between the couple, like a static electric field or a bad connection.

There are techniques to prevent this kind of interference, tantric exercises that can help a couple create a positive atmosphere for their relationship. We refer to this positive atmosphere as *harmony*. Harmony is a condition of balance—the balance of positive and negative energy, of electric and magnetic qualities, of light and dark properties, of inward and outward directedness. Most of us know harmony as a wonderful feeling of peacefulness, of rightness. But most of us believe it is a kind of blessed visitation, not something we can manufacture, let alone sustain.

But we can manufacture it; and it is to this manufacture of harmony that the tantric couple dedicates itself. Harmony can be created through communication. And just as Tantra endows male and female attributes with qualities far beyond mere genetic differences, so it ascribes to communication a lot more than mere talk. Tantric couples communicate with all their senses and on many levels: They connect physically, mentally, and spiritually—some would say psychically. A tantric couple establishes what we don't hesitate to call a "holy communion."

CREATING HARMONY:
THE NURTURING MEDITATION

The nurturing meditation is one of the simplest yet most profound of the tantric secrets for sustaining love's energy in a relationship. It is a physical form of communication that Tantricas practice at least twice a day. For most western couples who are apart during the day, this exercise is usually performed in the morning before they get out of bed, at the end of the work day when they reunite, and/or before they go to sleep. This connection may or may not be sexual; its goal is strictly to nurture one another and to exchange intimacy and energy. Too often couples engage in "all or nothing" sex. Either they "do it," and go all the way, or they don't do anything at all. For some reason many couples seem to think that the joy of passionate kissing, of touching one another, means one thing only, and must lead to one thing only. Often the nurturing meditation creates an attitude in the partners and an atmosphere around them that makes them both more open to a sexual union than they might have been before it. If time permits, many couples continue this ritual to a complete sexual expression. But sex is not the goal of this particular communication, and it should not be the expectation.

To practice the nurturing meditation, couples assume the "nurturing position." They lie together spoon-fashion on their left sides (for reasons of energy flow, according to the tantric texts). The partner on the inside is enveloped in the arms of the partner on the outside. Sometimes the man will be on the inside enveloped by the woman, sometimes the woman will be on the inside enveloped by the man; whoever feels most in need of nurturing, whoever has experienced the most stress that day, or is the most tired, should take the inside.

The purpose of this nurturing position is to create the balance necessary for harmony, to influence a synchronicity between the partners, to adjust their separate energies so that they are vibrating on the same frequency. Tucked together this way, with their chakras aligned front to back, the two bodies tune one another. Their separate energy centers regulate one to the other, and balance between the partners is achieved. The position will vary slightly from couple to couple, because of preferences and the size and shape of the partners, but in all cases comfort is essential. Neither person should experience any strain, or persist in a position that is the slightest bit uncomfortable. If the woman is holding the man, her right hand might rest on his belly (third chakra) or on his genitals (second chakra); her left arm might slip under the crook of his neck (the weight of his head borne by a pillow so her arm is free to move) and her left hand might rest on his chest (fourth chakra), or on his forehead (sixth chakra).

As you lie together, close your eyes and relax. Quiet your mind by focusing on deep breathing. Concentrate on the path of your breath as it rises up into and then down out of your nostrils. After a while, become aware of your partner's breath. Two breathing techniques are performed in this position. The first, used during the first few minutes of the meditation, is called the *harmonizing breath:* the couple inhales together, holds the breath together, exhales together, and holds the breath out together. During this harmonizing breath the partner on the inside is the receptive body, accepting energy through the back and into the chakras, filling up with that energy on each inhalation. The partner on the outside is the giver, and should emphasize each exhalation, projecting the chakras' energy from the front of the body into the receptive back side of the beloved. Practice three whole breaths (inhaling, holding in, exhaling, holding out) at each chakra, beginning at the heart center. Focus attention on the brow chakra next, then on the base chakra. From there concentrate on each of the other chakras in ascending order, bypassing the heart and brow chakras already visited. It is important for both partners to focus on the same chakra region at the same time.

The second breathing technique, used during the second part of the nurturing exercise, is called the *reciprocal charging breath.* This time one partner breathes in as the other partner breathes out. In this way during the several seconds that the breath is held, one partner will be holding the breath in, the other holding the breath out. As you practice the reciprocal charging breath, be conscious of the energy your partner is imparting to you as well as the energy you are giving back.

The nurturing meditation allows couples to communicate on at least three levels: on the conscious level, skin to skin; on the more subtle respiratory level, breath to breath; and on the most subtle level, chakra to chakra. Over time such regular communication creates a kind of synergy between the partners' chakras.

As you become familiar with the use of yantras, you may use them in this practice by visualizing them as you experience your chakras' energy. And if you add tantric touching to the nurturing meditation, an even deeper connection is possible. (See Chapter Eight, The Dance of Love, for touching techniques.)

The focus on breath and on energy centers seems to create its own energy. Certainly when partners complete this meditative posture, they each hold more energy than when they first joined together. When you start each day with the nurturing meditation, you not only charge your partner with part of yourself and in that way reaffirm your relationship, you also begin your day with love, creating a wonderful mood to get up into, and providing yourself with extra energy for whatever the day requires.

When you have completed this meditation (it should last about ten minutes), use another tantric means of communication before you go on to whatever is next on your agenda (fixing breakfast or dinner, talking to the kids, etc.). Look at one another. Look *into* one another. Don't speak; just gaze upon the face of your partner with whom you now feel so well connected. Notice the light that radiates from your lover's eyes; it is another by-product of the nurturing meditation—the light of love when harmony exists.

In addition to the nurturing meditation we have described, couples should enjoy a ritualistic meeting of minds, so to speak, in a shared five-minute-a-day sitting meditation. You can use yantras or mantras to focus your minds together, or any form of meditation or prayer. Many couples find it most satisfying to practice this focusing of the minds together at the end of the work day. They can then slide right into the nurturing meditation, which becomes a sort of "happy hour" for them.

It doesn't really matter when you practice these meditations, but it is essential that you make them part of your regular daily routine. They are keys to achieving harmony.

THE COUPLE AS A TEAM

The tantric books look upon a couple as equal partners in a relationship, as teammates, which is quite astounding when we consider that tantric yoga has been around for thousands of years, while for us the idea of "equal partners" is a fairly new concept.

So we are teammates, sharing a life, which is our "playing field," in a relationship that is the "game." To continue the metaphor, it would seem obvious that the teammates in this game ought to be playing by the same rules, but many couples are not. Many operate under different assumptions, and many don't even know what the rules are.

By "rules" we don't mean a stringent set of laws that dictate how things must be, or who must do what—we've just referred to a relationship as a game, after all, not a jail term. But even games are defined by parameters, and that's what each relationship needs to achieve—a mutual understanding of what the game is all about, of what the parameters are. Is it a summer romance, or are you building a future together? What do you want from your partner? What is your role? What is your partner's role? Who is the quarterback? Who is calling the plays? Is this the game you thought you signed up for? Do you enjoy it?

The general parameters you set may, of course, be changed as your relationship changes, but never unilaterally. You and your partner must redefine them together. And there is one Golden Rule that can never be changed. You and your partner must preserve harmony in your relationship by communicating and sharing on an intimate level. You can do this sexually, of course, but there are other ways, too. The nurturing meditation, for example, provides an invaluable sharing experience in which to exchange your most deeply generated energies. Some couples jog together, or bicycle together, or take long walks together as a demonstration of their shared investment in a healthy body and a healthy relationship.

Tantric couples share mentally, too. They meditate together, they share their thoughts, dreams, fears, hopes, and fantasies. And they work together. We are perhaps unusual in that we share a career, but our seminars are filled with couples who have learned to share other work—couples who do the dishes together, or garden together, or clean out the garage as a team. Many find that after practicing the art of conscious loving for a while, they are inspired to create new projects together. No matter what work you do as a couple, collaboration is the cornerstone of a good relationship because it endows the partnership with the unique productive quality that comes from working together. Working together on a project or at a job is symbolic of working on the relationship—paying attention to it, and in so doing, paying it homage. As you work together as a team, whether on a mundane chore or on an inspired creative endeavor, you are also working together toward the goal of harmony, that honeyed atmosphere in which love grows and passion is an eternal flame. Teammates help each other out for the sake of harmony. Where one is weak, the other provides strength. The couple cover for one another, support one another. They are teammates; they are pals. They build each other up, they *never* put each other down—they know that to hurt one's partner is to hurt oneself.

This is an important lesson to assimilate and put into practice. But it's not always easy, especially when your partner has done or said something you consider hurtful, and which seems to demonstrate a confused mind, or unconsciousness, or simple thoughtlessness. One of the tantric disciplines addresses just this sort of situation and suggests a method of speech, a way of talking to one another—even in adversity—without blame. We'll take a look at this technique in the next chapter.

FOUR

TANTRIC COMMUNICATION

Think before thou speakest.

CERVANTES, *Don Quixote de la Mancha*, part IV, book 3

Conscious loving requires conscious communication. This does not mean that you have to learn a new vocabulary (although most of the couples who come to our seminars do leave with a few Sanskrit words that become a part of their shared "secret" language, like pet names do), but it does mean that you must be aware of what you are saying and that you must learn a ritual method of communication with your partner. When you are hurt, or angry, or insecure, you need to communicate your feelings to your partner (bad feelings that aren't aired can become infectious in a relationship), but you need to watch your words in doing so. You need to avoid blaming your partner for your own feelings.

Watching one's language with a close partner, however, is not an easy thing to do. Somehow it's easier to be careful about what we say when we're among strangers than it is when we're with the person we love. Somehow we believe that one of the comforts of the close partnership is not having to watch every word. And while the tantric doctrines don't say "watch every word," precisely, they do say that you must be conscious of your method of communication and conscious of how your words may be interpreted. This is especially important for couples, because intimates not only know how to give one another pleasure, they also know how to inflict pain. Admittedly, painful remarks are most often made "unconsciously," like a Freudian slip, but they are no less potent, no less destructive than if they had been spoken with malice aforethought.

Tantra requires of its students a certain level of awareness to avoid the disharmony that results from thoughtless communication.

DISHARMONY

Let's face it, no matter how good our intentions, no matter how hard we try, disharmony occurs. We are influenced by things outside of us as well as inside—we are human. We get out of sync with our partner. We get angry, hurt, hassled. Sometimes we get bored. Disharmony in and of itself is not a bad thing. In fact, the tantric books consider the occurrence of disharmony an important part of a relationship, and necessary for its growth and health. The partners are, after all, inherently opposite, and they are both complex beings, with personal conflicts and individual contradictions and uncertainties. On top of that, they are both in a constant state of change, of growth and evolution; who they are today may be different from, possibly even the opposite of, who they were and who they may become. That being so, their combination as a couple is bound to be at least as complex as they are individually; the odds of an occasional miscombination are high. There really is no one to blame for disharmony when it occurs, and without it our notion of its opposite would pale. But since love languishes in disharmony, the tantric couple, devoted to their love, takes immediate steps to change the atmosphere and restore harmony. They do this by taking love into their hurt places. They use their love to replace disharmony with harmony and in this way they heal the injured partnership.

The tantric lesson on the subject of conflict in a relationship uses the metaphor of an archer whose arrow will move forward only if he pulls back against his bow. It is the contraction (or when we talk about a couple, their contraction, their pulling away from each other in opposition) and the subsequent release of tension that propels the arrow (and the couple) on a forward-moving path.

Some couples who "contract" or experience disharmony may let an argument simmer along until the heat drives one of them out. One person physically leaves the scene of such bad energy—takes a walk around the block, for instance, to cool off. Some couples accelerate the simmer to a boil with acrimonious words and actions. Some couples don't engage in any confrontation at all, which, for its explosive potential, may be the most dangerous course, even though it seems the most civilized. In any of these cases the result is an energetic fission, whether it occurs out in the open or inside. Where there was harmony there is now a vacuum that feels like a black hole in space. Love cannot live in a vacuum, and when two lovers have fallen into this metaphorical black hole, they are like the negative poles of magnets; they are in opposition, unattracted. Their chakra systems are operating on incompatible frequencies, actually repelling one another.

A master archer will let go of his arrow as soon as his contraction is complete and his aim is taken. In the same way a Tantrica knows that to hold onto contraction or disharmony beyond a certain point expends needless energy and strains both partners to no advantage. The tantric couple, bound by the rule that harmony is paramount to their relationship and must be restored, is committed to "letting go" as soon as possible. As long as the partners continue their argument, engaging their throat chakras in a verbal expression of opposition, they will not effect a cure, solve the problem, or restore peace. In fact, nothing will be accomplished until someone lets go.

Before we discuss how tantric communication can help contemporary couples let go of an argument, we need to talk about the nature of disharmony. We have learned from the couples we meet in our seminars that most arguments or disagreements stem from and escalate out of the fact that one partner is communicating logically, the other emotionally. We use a classic story about a modern-day couple to demonstrate this duality: Following a conversation in which Linda and Sam regret the dwindling amount of spontaneity in their relationship, Linda plans a romantic evening as a surprise. She sends the kids off to a neighbor's for the night and prepares Sam's favorite foods for dinner. In the flush of anticipation she splurges on a sheer, sexy, pale blue chemise that she knows will drive Sam crazy.

Meanwhile, Sam's boss asks him to work late on a special project that afternoon. Linda is out when he calls, and she's forgotten to turn on the answering machine. Involved in his project, Sam doesn't remember to call again until he's about to leave the office at seven o'clock, and then the line is busy. Rather than wait to get through, he leaves work and heads for home. Naturally, he gets caught in traffic.

By the time Sam walks in the door he is frazzled by the freeway, hungry, tired, and looking forward to the comforts of home. For about a minute. Something is obviously wrong with Linda; she's cold and uncommunicative. She's been crying, Sam thinks, and he asks her what's wrong.

But Linda doesn't want to talk—she can hardly look at Sam, she's so hurt. Perhaps his "not being there" has triggered subtle memories of other men who weren't there when she wanted them— her father, for example. Or maybe she experiences the situation as a humiliation that resonates with previous hurts. Whatever the underlying cause, she's upset and she's emotional. If Sam persists in an interrogation about what's wrong, Linda might say, "You ruined everything—my surprise, everything." Or, "It means nothing to you that I went to all this trouble. You didn't even call. You have no respect for my feelings. You're just selfish. You made me worry. You ruined our dinner." And then she might begin to cry.

Linda is blaming Sam for her feelings: "You made me worry," instead of "I worried." "You have no respect," instead of "I feel disrespected." But it would do no good to point this out to her now.

Sam explains that he did try to call, but the answering machine wasn't on. He points out that he had no idea she was planning a surprise, that she is very important to him, that she has no reason to be angry with him, and that she shouldn't cry.

When Linda hears Sam say that she shouldn't be angry and shouldn't cry, she takes it to mean that Sam believes she is wrong for feeling what she feels. The fact that Sam is judging her to be wrong (which by implication means that he is right) is infuriating and disappointing to her at the same time, and her emotional distress accelerates.

The more emotional Linda becomes, the harder Sam tries to reason with her, but Linda, in an emotional mindset, isn't being reasonable. Sam is still hungry and tired, and now he feels unappreciated, misunderstood, and beat up. He tells Linda he is going out for a hamburger and that while he's gone she should try to get hold of herself.

Linda's fears of abandonment are now approaching emergency level and Sam is at the end of his rope. It may be days before this couple recovers their connectedness, days before they communicate intimately again. Unless it is cleared, the residue of this conflict will recede to a corner of their psyches, where it will wait in the shadows until the next blow to either of their insecurities brings it back into the light.

We call this a classic example of duality because it demonstrates what happens when a couple speaks two different languages: neither can "get" what the other is trying to say. In our example we assign Sam the logical, yang, or masculine voice, and Linda the emotional, yin, or feminine voice, but of course the roles are often reversed. The fact remains, however, that as long as couples speak from these two disparate frames of reference, they cannot reach agreement. The logical partner will remain certain about the "rightness" of his or her convictions, because they make perfect sense. The emotional partner will continue in his or her position because the truth of feelings cannot be denied.

THREE STEPS
TOWARD RESTORING HARMONY

In this kind of contraction, where emotion and logic are at odds, it serves nothing for the rational person to attempt to explain anything rationally. The emotional person doesn't need to be convinced at this moment—in fact, *can't* be convinced, because that requires a logical mind and for now the emotional mind is in charge. The emotional partner wants only to be heard, held, and loved; only wants harmony restored. When Sam advises Linda to get hold of herself, he is on the right track—she needs to be held.

If Sam had recognized this need, he could have assumed the role of master archer and initiated a harmonic meditation. This is the first step toward restoring harmony. Whichever partner becomes aware of what's happening first—realizes through the dark cloud of a disagreement that harmony has been obliterated and that the loving partnership is endangered—that person must let go, must say something like, "Listen, we're not connecting," or "We're not in harmony. I don't think we can solve this by talking any more. We can finish this discussion later when we're not so upset."

The second step is for the person who has been able to let go of the argument to suggest that the partners lie down together and practice the nurturing meditation as a means of getting back together and restoring harmony. We realize that the nurturing meditation is the last thing you want to do in the middle of a fight, so it's one of the "rules," one of the "commitments" that tantric teammates agree to beforehand. Remember, the maintenance of harmony in your relationship is the first consideration. Whatever else is going on, the individual partners consider themselves subordinate to that. Further, Tantricas understand that mental, emotional, or physical reconciliation cannot be achieved between partners until their *energy* is reconciled. In an argument, it is almost as if the chakras blow a circuit. So even though you may feel an energetic repulsion, you lie down together in the nurturing position.

Immediately the situation changes. A new element is added that dilutes the atmosphere, changes its concentration. Sam may continue to think that Linda is stubborn, or childish, for example, but now he is aware of her body, even though this awareness may be of the negative physical energy she is still generating. Sam may feel no attraction for Linda at this point, but his conscious effort to restore

42

harmony qualifies not only as an act of solidarity, a demonstration of his dedication to the relationship, but also as an act of meditation because he is consciously turning his focus from an intellectual mode of disagreement to a passive physical and energetic form of communication. Linda, too, begins to consciously focus on Sam, communicating with him passively rather than emotionally. The couple becomes conscious of their breathing. They notice that their breath is very shallow and/or quick. This is because the respiratory system seems to shut down to a degree under duress, perhaps in an effort to protect the subtle body beneath. Linda and Sam consciously begin to breathe more slowly and deeply. They adjust their breath to each other and begin to breathe as one.

Once a couple has matched their breathing, the harmonic adjustment begins almost immediately. Within five minutes most couples will have corrected the problem of their chakras operating on incompatible frequencies. On that subtle level they will have created a reconciliation. They will not have resolved their dispute, of course, but they will be together again, and together is the only way they will ultimately settle the disagreement.

Think of Linda and Sam the next time you and your partner have an argument, and try the nurturing meditation as a method for restoring harmony. Go through the entire meditation, and as the two of you begin to feel together again, as your chakras become more compatible again, consciously try to feel your togetherness and the harmony of it. Face one another and make a connection with your eyes. Don't say anything; communicate only with the light of each other's eyes. You may find that you understand the situation differently now, or that it has diminished in importance. Nevertheless, in no case should you pursue an intellectual coming-to-terms at this time. Agree to talk about it the next day when you are not under the influence of anger or hurt. If it is a subject on which you have disagreed before, it may be a good idea to have your discussion with a trusted counselor or friend present. A third party can help keep the discussion on track, and couples often communicate with one another more carefully when someone else is there.

Once the nurturing meditation has taken effect and you and your partner feel more together, it is time to initiate step three, a ritual communication we call "no-fault language." In this verbal recitation of love and forgiveness, both partners express sorrow for their part in the disagreement, and affirm their love and their desire to restore harmony. Then each partner forgives the other for his or her part in the argument. This may seem contrived, but ritual is a contrivance that communicates on a much deeper level than the actual words do. In this ritual the partners are acknowledging that their disagreement belongs to both of them, that each owns a part of it, and that love and forgiveness and mutual harmony have the strength to quiet and calm it.

THE 3-STEP METHOD
FOR RESTORING HARMONY

1. Let go.
2. Reconnect through the
   nurturing meditation.
3. Communicate with no-fault
   language.

If you find yourself slipping back into the argument when you begin to speak, or if you find no light in your partner's eyes, do not pursue any verbal communication. You will not resolve your dispute today, and the best you can do is to get back in tune on a physical level. *Hold each other longer. The gesture is both a literal and a figurative way to hold onto your love.* You will achieve a balance with your lover in this nurturing position. It really works. Even though you are at odds intellectually and emotionally, your subtle body systems cannot help but be affected by the energetic synchronization you achieve in this exercise. The level of balance varies, however, and if it's too delicate, or if your argument is a symptom of something bigger than itself, the harmony you manufacture may continue to dissolve and need to be restored until you have dealt with whatever the real problem is. Don't push your newly restored harmony—wait to tackle problems until both partners are feeling positive and strong, not when you've only just established an uneasy or uncertain truce.

But what about couples who have grown apart, who are no longer compatible on any level, and who have tried marital counseling to no avail? Will the three-step method work for them? Probably not. When love no longer exists between partners, it can't very well be revived. For couples who have lost each other in this way, harmony may be impossible to achieve, or it may be fleeting and impermanent. The death of love is a loss as painful as any passing, and we believe it is often best to acknowledge it as one does any other death, by burying it ritually and moving on with one's life.

For the vast majority of couples we work with, however, love still exists and they are looking for the means to secure it, deepen it, sustain it. These men and women report back to us that the three-step method for restoring harmony refreshes them and supports them even in their differences. Prove it to yourself. The next time you and your partner are at odds with one another, remember the Golden Rule that harmony reign, and let go of the argument. Then assume the nurturing position with your partner and begin the meditation. Finally, as you feel your bodies coming together again, speak the no-fault language ritual to each other. Personalize the process for yourselves by using words of your own choosing, and by creating your own variations. In our own relationship, for example, we have found it helpful to grant each other a "one-time refusal clause." In other words, if one of us is ready to make up but the other is still "stuck," the one who is not ready may refuse to reconcile for a period of ten or fifteen minutes. Then, before we engage in the nurturing meditation, the still-angry or still-hurt person takes a shower, after which he or she assumes the receptive, inside position in the nurturing meditation. (The shower is important; Tantricas use a ritual bath to refresh themselves "body and soul." People are always amazed at how quickly this changes energy levels in the direction of reharmonization.)

GIFTS OF LOVE

While the three-step method can help *restore* harmony to a relationship that has been temporarily disrupted, there is another important form of communication that, practiced regularly, can help *maintain* harmony. Love is often described as the greatest of gifts—perhaps because of the mystery of it. We don't know where it comes from; we can't even do a very good job of defining it. To demonstrate their perception of love as a gift, and to communicate their appreciation for it, Tantricas make frequent gifts to one another. These gifts can be material, tangible expressions of love. Flowers, for example, have been used for just such ceremonial purposes in all cultures, in every age. They are perfect gifts for couples to offer each other; symbols of life and growth, they bring with them fragrance, color, and beauty. Gifts can also be expressed verbally—"I love you," or "You look terrific." Or they can be something as valuable as diamonds. Like much of the tantric arts and rituals, the act of giving a token of love is symbolic of something greater. For tantric lovers, gifts are offerings, and the act of giving is an act of honoring, of paying homage, which is quite like an act of worship.

Gifts of love can be custom-fitted to bring joy to the recipient, and because they are symbolic they can be the simplest things. Partners may surprise one another with theater tickets, for instance, or a dinner out; they may leave love notes in unexpected places. One may cook a favorite meal for the other, give a massage or a shampoo, or wash the other's car.

Compromise can also be considered a gift, and it most definitely can be an expression of love. For example, she goes skiing with him even though she'd rather be out shopping or home reading; he goes dancing with her, even though he'd much prefer to be home watching a sports event on TV. Compromise—even concession—takes on a whole new meaning when one's highest goal is harmony. Tantricas know they can never *make* another person happy, but they can supply their intimate partner with many *reasons to feel happy and loved.* This is considered a sacred duty of each partner. So indulge one another every day if you can, but certainly make your dearest partner a love gift every week.

FIVE

TANTRIC HEALING

Lead me from the unreal to the real!
Lead me from darkness to light!
Lead me from death to immortality!

Brihadaranyaka Upanishad

We have spoken of how the tantric practices address us on the physical, intellectual, and spiritual levels. There are aspects of Tantra that speak to qualities found on each of these levels. In our study of the tantric texts, we have found that extrapolation from Tantra's healing aspects can be useful as a therapy for what we might refer to as psychosexual wounds.

We use the word "extrapolation" because the kind of healing tantric couples needed five thousand years ago—in this area, anyway—is not comparable with the healing we of the modern age require. The early Hindu practitioners of tantric yoga experienced and taught sexual play and sexual union as an act of joyful celebration, as a demonstration of connectedness, as a symbolic affirmation of the unity inherent in a couple's relationship, and as a means for achieving spiritual sublimity. The art of sexual love was the noblest of sixty-five arts and sciences a dedicated Tantrica aspired to master. So sexual "hangups" were not prevalent, and tantric "healing" meant something quite different from what we mean when we apply it to couples today.

It's interesting that the tantric books refer to our age—this turn-of-the-century period—as part of the Age of Darkness, *Kali Yuga* in Sanskrit, and the reference is quite specific regarding our era's primitive sexual evolutionary status. Vedic scripture (a profound body of Hindu philosophy and scholarship) also identifies this time as the Age of Darkness and describes it as a period "when society reaches a stage where property confers rank, wealth becomes the only source of virtue...falsehood the source of success in life... and when outer trappings are confused with inner religion."

Fortunately, by the same calendar, we are at the very edge of this darkness, in the very last years of this age, and about to reenter the Age of Truth, or *Satya Yuga*. And we do see evidence that we are moving in that direction. There seem to be more of us who are making an effort to know ourselves and one another better, who desire to cast light on whatever darkness exists inside ourselves, and who seek to light a path for others, to make a positive difference in this world, whether with a partner or alone.

THE SIXTY-FOUR "OTHER" ARTS
(Adapted from *The Kama Sutra of Vatsyayana*)

1. Singing
2. Playing musical instruments
3. Dancing
4. The union of dancing, singing, and playing instrumental music
5. Writing and drawing
6. Tattooing
7. Arraying and adorning an idol with rice and flowers
8. Spreading and arranging flowers
9. Coloring the teeth, garments, hair, nails, and body
10. Fixing stained glass into a floor
11. Making beds, and spreading out carpets and cushions for reclining
12. Playing on musical glasses filled with water
13. Storing and accumulating water in aqueducts, cisterns, and reservoirs
14. Picture making, trimming, and decorating
15. Stringing rosaries, necklaces, garlands, and wreaths

16. Binding of turbans and chaplets, and making crests and top-knots of flowers
17. Scenic representations, stage playing
18. Making ear ornaments
19. Preparing perfumes and odors
20. Proper disposition of jewels and decorations, and adornment in dress
21. Magic of sorcery
22. Quickness of hand or manual skill
23. Culinary art
24. Making lemonades, sherbets, acidulated drinks, and spiritous extracts with proper flavor and color
25. Tailor's work and sewing
26. Making parrots, flowers, tufts, tassels, bunches, bosses, knobs, etc. out of yarn or thread
27. Solving riddles, verbal puzzles, and enigmatical questions
28. Skill in a verse game, which requires one player to begin a verse with a word that starts with the same letter with which the last player's verse ended
29. Art of mimicry or imitation
30. Reading, including chanting and intoning
31. Study of sentences difficult to pronounce—played as a game chiefly by women and children
32. Practice with sword, singlestick, quarterstaff, and bow and arrow
33. Drawing inferences, reasoning, or inferring
34. Carpentry
35. Architecture
36. Knowledge about gold and silver coins, jewels, and gems
37. Chemistry and mineralogy
38. Coloring jewels, gems, and beads
39. Knowledge of mines and quarries
40. Gardening
41. Cock fighting, quail fighting, and ram fighting

42. Teaching parrots and starlings to speak

43. Applying perfumed ointments to the body, and dressing the hair with unguents and perfumes and braiding it

44. Understanding writing in cypher

45. Speaking by changing the forms of words

46. Knowledge of a language and of the vernacular dialects

47. Making flower carriages

48. Framing mystical diagrams, addressing spells and charms, and binding armlets

49. Mental exercises, such as completing stanzas or verses on receiving just a part of them, or putting into verse or prose sentences represented by signs or symbols

50. Composing poems

51. Knowledge of dictionaries and vocabularies

52. Knowledge of the ways of changing and disguising the appearance of persons

53. Knowledge of the ways of changing the appearance of things, such as making cotton to appear as silk

54. Various ways of gambling

55. Art of obtaining possession of the property of others by means of mantras or incantations

56. Skill in youthful sports

57. Knowledge of the rules of society, and of how to pay respect and compliments to others

58. Knowledge of the art of war

59. Knowledge of gymnastics

60. Knowing the character of a man from his features

61. Knowledge of scanning or constructing verses

62. Arithmetical recreations

63. Making artificial flowers

64. Making figures and images in clay

SEX IN THE AGE OF DARKNESS

Let us try now to cast light on some of the problems we children of the Dark Age are facing. We'll begin with the mixed messages we received about sex from childhood on. Most boys, for example, notice at a very young age how good sex feels through masturbation, and most are told in no uncertain terms not to do it. Most religions attempt to regulate sex with laws telling us how and when it may be practiced, and with dire penalties for those who disobey these laws. Our *bodies* make no moral judgment on sex, but many of us absorb the vision of our church or our parents, and whether or not we continue to accept this vision as true, we still carry with us the message that, except under special circumstances, *sex is bad*. Even during the sexual revolution, when a comparatively uninhibited sexual freedom was practiced, many individuals remained uncertain of the "rightness" of this freedom. It is not easy to expunge a previous generation's lessons in a decade or two.

As a result, there are a lot of people in the prime of their sexual years—from thirty to sixty years old—walking around with a vaguely guilty past, whether real or imagined. When you attach guilt, which is defined as "the state of having committed an offense or crime against moral or penal law," to sexuality, you make it offensive and criminal. And just as guilt often carries a measure of remorse with it, so may sex. Those who suffer with the "subtle knowledge" that what they are doing is wrong because they aren't married, or because they are not procreating, or on even deeper levels, because they feel unworthy of the kind of pleasure to be experienced from sex, are likely to feel both guilty and remorseful.

Furthermore, with the onslaught of AIDS, we have come to associate sex with the possibility of disease. Of course, this is not a new phenomenon; venereal diseases have been around for centuries. But we were born lucky; modern medicine gave us the means to avoid serious sexual infections—until AIDS.

Another characteristic we associate with sex is shame. We learn when we are very young not to talk about or touch our genitals in public. It's okay to talk about other body parts, but not those of the second chakra. Even our healing arts, even conscious, holistic practitioners, avoid addressing the sexual center. Massage, for instance, is acceptable when applied to any part of the body other than the sexual areas.

Among the couples we work with, we find many negative imprints attached to these sexual areas. Both women and men, for example, have negative associations regarding menstruation. Some men are uneasy, even queasy, about the whole idea of it. For women, there may be an association with physical pain, with a fear of embarrassment, of "accidents," with the emotional tides that sometimes accompany menstruation. All of us associate loss of blood with injury and trauma, and no one feels good about that. Involuntary erections and premature ejaculations can make men feel out of control and insecure. Orgasm itself is an uncontrolled physical spasm. And we have all worried about the appearance of our sexual parts at one time or another. Is it too big, or too small? Are they the right shape? Is there an odor?

Many of us also learned the truly perverse axiom that "nice girls don't do it." Boys were taught that the only kind of girl they were supposed to "love" (as in marry or have a serious relationship with) was one of those nice ones who didn't. Girls got the same message, and were therefore horrified (or pretended to be) when a boy tried to touch them—What kind of girl does he think I am? Obviously, "love" excluded sex and vice versa.

Even though we may recognize this as an old program, most of us still carry these data within ourselves. In most cases this inappropriate indoctrination doesn't prevent us from finding a partner and being a lover; but even when we reject the original data the old programming occasionally flares up, becoming a subtle factor in the way we see ourselves, in our sexuality, and in our relationships. Even if our sexual history doesn't cause overt problems, it can have a covert effect on our ability to project love and to feel love through the sexual center.

As if these enormous negative imprints on the issue of sexuality were not enough of an encumbrance, we of this Age of Darkness are further burdened by the fact that we are uneducated in sex. Unlike the eastern Tantricas of days past, we come to our sexual awakening awkwardly, fearfully, and very much in the dark. Even sophisticated, sexually experienced, well-educated, otherwise worldly people operate on fallacious sexual assumptions and misinformation. Many of us never realize, even after years of sexual relationships, the full potential possible in sexual union.

In addition to all of these factors, which are really just a composite layer of influence that is to a major degree *external,* we are toting around an *internal* personal memory record that is even more immediate than our cultural indoctrination. These personal sexual experiences may have disappointed, or hurt, or frightened us far more than they provided us joy. According to the tantric books, these experiences are as much a symptom of the Age of Darkness as they are a product of the individual.

Obviously, all this negativity is going to have a negative effect on our present and future sexuality. The application of tantric principles can eliminate the scars etched by our sexual history, both personal and cultural. Time and again we have seen this happen, because Tantra addresses negativity on the very deepest levels. It encompasses every yin, or dark, aspect of it and matches it with its opposite yang, or light, quality. Tantric yoga is a balancing act. When disharmony occurs the tantric couple makes a purposeful, conscious revision in the atmosphere by balancing their bodies' opposing or negative impulses. When Tantricas exchange sexual love, they draw on their separate impulse centers or bodily chakras to balance yin and yang, feminine and masculine, negative and positive. In the same way, balance can be achieved for the negative sexual histories we bring to a relationship. Tantra directly addresses the area where psychic or physical injury may exist. It uses love as a salve, as a tonic, as a panacea for sexual wounds.

LIGHT HEALING

It is not easy to image a system of therapy—Freudian, Jungian, or gestalt, group or individual—that doesn't require, for openers, shining light on the problem. Lighting something is a very yang, or positive, gesture that immediately affects a negative situation. Tantra asserts that negative imprints from sexual preconceptions and past experiences make their home in the region of the second chakra, just as injuries sustained by ambition or fear rest in the third chakra, and heartbreaks in the fourth, and tantric healing requires that we address the afflicted chakra directly.

The first step toward healing our sexual scars is to shine light on the second chakra so we can "see" what is creating the short circuit, or the block, or fear, or coldness, or anger, or just plain craziness. We use tantric meditation techniques to make the light— to create an atmosphere we can see through, one that is radiant, that has the power to uplift us and move us through the darkness. In Chapter Two we discussed a number of techniques for focusing the mind; any of these techniques can be used to achieve a meditative state, which is the first source of light because it lifts us out of our lower selves and into a higher mindset. Once we have achieved that state, we focus on the second chakra. The yantra or design symbol of the second chakra is a cradle-crescent moon within a circle (see the chart on page 18). Imagine that design painted on a door and imagine that this door opens into a room filled with your personal sexual belongings. You must enter this room with a lantern held high against the darkness. You must walk through the room, past everything in it, in order to overcome your personal obstacles; each time you enter here with light, you will eradicate a little bit of darkness.

Western therapies require the individual to enter this room of preconceptions and past experiences alone. One can visualize a spirit guide, one may have the support of a therapist or counselor on the way, but the journey through the room must be made alone. Tantric yoga exhorts the couple to make the journey *together*. Their combined strength makes for an easier opening of those doors within themselves, and their opposite natures help them balance and heal each other.

PARTNERS AS HEALERS

When partners are healers to each other, when they create light inside each other as a kind of radiation therapy for pain or fear or distrust, they make a profound connection. This connection involves two forms of energy: the energy of intimacy and the energy of sexual passion. These are the two main ingredients in tantric loving.

Tantric texts identify the fourth or heart chakra, which is the seat of intimacy, as a center of distinctly retrograde energy for men and progressive energy for women. The man's fourth chakra may be pictured as a wheel spinning in a counterclockwise direction, while the woman's is spinning clockwise. His is in a state of reversion, hers is capable of conversion. This is the nature of men and women, say the ancient writings. Because of this, for most men psychosexual difficulties and negative sexual imprints lodged in the second chakra find a compatible negative atmosphere in the fourth chakra, and often translate into difficulty in achieving and expressing intimacy.

On the other hand the second chakra, home of sexual energy and motivation, is a center of retrograde energy for women, while for men it is a focal point for transmutable power. So negative sexual propaganda is drawn to a woman's negative second center and lodges there as difficulty in expressing herself sexually, and often as difficulty in achieving a satisfying sexuality at all.

So here we are, men and women, each proficient in an area of deficiency in the other. In combination, in balance, the couple can nullify deficiency by teaching one another the secrets of their separate strengths. They can use the art, science, and ritual of tantric lovemaking to achieve a powerful healing yoga, or union—to open doors to one another, for one another, and for the relationship itself. This yoga can replace dark memories with a bright present, create

57

a new understanding of the meaning of sex and sexuality and partnership, and banish jealousy, possessiveness, and other ghosts of the past in the face of the absolute self-assurance the tantric couple gains in the practice of the art.

PART II

SEXUAL PLEASURE: ACHIEVING THE ECSTATIC IN LOVE

SIX

AWAKENING THE GODDESS

The valley spirit never dies;
It is the woman, primal mother.
Her gateway is the root of heaven and earth...

LAO TSU, *Tao Te Ching*, number 6

In the last chapter we noted that tantric books describe our age as the end of the Kali Yuga, or Age of Darkness, a period that began more than two thousand years ago. The Kali Yuga has been marked by corruption and difficulty, and, according to the tantric texts, it has been an era during which female power has been suppressed. Metaphorically, the Hindu Goddess Shakti, who represents the female principle, has lain sleeping for over two millennia. There are various theories about the Goddess's slumber. One explanation is that man became frightened by the intensity of woman's *shakti,* or energetic power, and by what she was capable of—creation, for one thing—so he maneuvered her into a subordinate position in order to suppress that power.

While historians differ as to the exact date when the Kali Yuga began, many authorities believe it was in the third and fourth centuries B.C., at about the same time that Taoism reached its apogee in China and Confucianism was gaining new popularity. What had been a fairly egalitarian political and social system in China began to change. Whereas previously emperor and empress had ruled as equals, now the emperor alone was sovereign. Similarly, in Taoist tantric lovemaking the man began to assume a new role. Where the original tantric techniques required an equal exchange between man and woman of positive and negative energies, of yang and yin, the beginning of the Age of Darkness found the man using his consort's energies for his own resources and longevity, without regard to her replenishment. No wonder the Goddess preferred to sleep.

Even earlier, in India, a similar male domination prevailed after the country was defeated by warrior tribes whose influence overwhelmed the predominantly matriarchal society. And so that force we call the *shakti,* which is personified by the Goddess, fell out of power and into the realm of dreams.

DAWN OF A NEW AGE

Now, as we stand on the cusp of a New Age, which Tantra calls Satya Yuga, the Age of Truth, we see the female fires beginning to glow again. We believe that the Goddess began her reawakening in the 1960s, during the period we know as the Sexual Revolution, and that she is still in the early stretching stages of waking up. Women's interest in physical fitness, in exercise and health, in self-improvement can be viewed as a literal manifestation of this stretching. Their expansion into business, politics, and spiritual pursuits is also a demonstration of their emergence as a new force in the modern world.

In fact, what we call the Women's Movement can be perceived as a dramatic play, an acting out of the Goddess awakening. It is movement up out of the subconscious. It is movement into the world. She opens her eyes. She shakes the Age of Darkness from her as she shakes off the dreams of centuries. Soon she will step out into the light, and her radiance will illuminate all humankind. When this happens, when women awake from their slumber and their enormous orgasmic energy is released to the world, we will have attained the New Age, the Age of Truth. For women themselves the difference will be as profound as the difference between night and day. ❀

Of course it's one thing to talk metaphorically, and quite another to speak in terms of reality. In reality this business of the Goddess awakening isn't such a simple thing. During two thousand and more years of suppression, women's fire has grown cold. Now suddenly it's the "New Age" and women are supposed to be more evolved on many levels, particularly on the sexual level. Not only are women expected to be having fabulous orgasms, they are also supposed to be experiencing multiple ones. It's enough to make anyone a little nervous, especially women who don't feel orgasms easily. "That's all well and good for the Goddess," a modern woman might say, "but what about me?"

The fact is, both men and women have to be taught how to rekindle the woman's dormant sexual energy. In the old days, Tantricas were tutored by teachers in the art of love, as well as the sixty-four other arts and sciences a disciple of Tantra was expected to know. Today, men and women can learn to teach each other, and Tantra can help them. They might consider Tantra as a kind of extension course—a master class in love and relationship. In this continuing education they guide each other, and the experience can be extremely powerful. For when a woman's fire is rekindled after such a long time, and tended, and fed by her most intimate partner, the benefits to both can be manifold. But for women, especially, the rekindling of dormant sexual fires can lead to startling, unexpected sensations. A woman's sexual awakening can, unlike a man's, propel her on a spiritual path. Men may practice celibacy and achieve spiritual enlightenment, but according to the tantric texts women's enlightenment is facilitated by the electric charge of her orgasmic nature. Through sexual sharing a woman activates a powerful sexual/spiritual energy, her shakti, which then releases itself into her physical body and into her psyche, creating the atmosphere for her awakening and spiritual enlightenment. Tantra recognizes spirituality as a kind of rearrangement of the same energy as sexuality, so when a woman increases her sexual power she adds, on an almost cellular level, to the strength of her spiritual aspect as well.

Once a woman is awakened, both partners benefit. The woman's pleasure and her desire for lovemaking increase and can even be *greater* than the pleasure potential and sexual desire in the man. Tantric lovemaking promotes health and vitality, and both the man and the woman benefit physically. Psychologically, too, Tantra is a healing art. We've discussed the various negative charges that can be associated with the second chakra, the energy center for the genitals—negative associations that can come from information our parents may have passed along, from our own hurtful past experiences, or from embarrassments we learned somewhere along our own particular path. Tantric practices can discharge the negative power infusing the second chakra, and in so doing make enormous resources of positive energy available to all areas of life, not just the sexual. You will discover an energy you never knew you had, a creative energy that will refresh your mind, replenish your stamina, and restore your enthusiasm.

FIVE LEVELS
OF ORGASMIC EXPERIENCE

When her sexual resources have been awakened and her passion fired, a woman can come to an orgasm in a minute or two if she so desires. Multiple orgasms are no longer a mere myth to her, and she discovers that her sexual energy (not the Goddess's sexual energy, but her own) is limitless.

We can identify five levels of orgasmic activity in women, beginning with the zero or *preorgasmic* level, which includes women who have never experienced an orgasm at all, as well as those who aren't sure. Women on this level may not have had the experience of making love, or perhaps they have never masturbated or have not been able to masturbate to climax. Perhaps they are sexually active but suffer a psychological block due to negative associations or previous incompatibilities. Or they may have been indoctrinated with the belief that nice girls shouldn't enjoy sex; or perhaps they are simply afraid of "losing control."

The second level, which we call *sometimes orgasmic,* can be much more frustrating than the preorgasmic level. To have experienced the feeling of an orgasm and not be able to call it up, not to have access to one's own power, can be intensely upsetting.

Next there is the *orgasmic* level. These women do have access to that potent energy. They have experienced orgasms and they know which positions and which combination of kisses and touches will induce it. And that's where women on this level are content to stop. "I've had my orgasm, dearest, and you've had yours. I love you. Good night."

Then there is the fourth level, *multiple orgasms,* like fireworks on the Fourth of July—there is that much color and intensity—a chain of pleasure possibility beyond the orgasmic stratosphere.

Beyond this is a fifth level, which sexologists call *extended orgasm* and Tantricas know as the Wave of Bliss. This is a level of arousal that grows in intensity and can last ten or twenty minutes or even longer. The tantric writings describe Shakti's achieving seven peaks of ecstasy, each peak higher, stronger, more powerful than the one preceding, until at the topmost place she releases her nectar, her *amrita,* the female ejaculate.

This is not a fairy tale. Every woman has such potential, but she must desire to awaken it, and she must desire it for *herself* first, not for her partner or his satisfaction.

ANATOMY OF A GODDESS:
A WOMAN'S TWO PLEASURE POLES

There has been a highly publicized debate recently about the existence of the Grafenberg Spot, or g spot. Freud started it, even before Mr. G, with his assertion that a clitoral orgasm is an immature orgasm, which suggests that there must be such a thing as a "mature" orgasm, achieved otherwise than through the clitoris. Psychologists went along with this theory for a while, defining two separate areas for the female orgasm, the clitoris and the vagina. Then in the 1960s, William Masters and Virginia Johnson, considered gurus in the field of sexology, superseded Freud's unfortunate phrase, maintaining that in fact the vaginal orgasm was a myth.

Female orgasm is achieved by stimulating the clitoris, they said, and that's all. There are stronger orgasms and weaker ones, but they all come from the same source. Today, many researchers dispute the Masters and Johnson theory. John Perry and Beverly Whipple, for example, agree that the clitoris is one point that may be stimulated to trigger a woman's orgasm, but they assert that it is not the only point.

Tantricas do not engage in this debate. They have known since Shiva pronounced it in the sacred books that inside a woman lie two sensitive poles, or charged spots, the northern or forward pole, which is the clitoris, and the deeper southern pole, called the *sacred spot,* which is the same as the g spot.

As we have noted, the tantric texts were written as a dialogue between the Hindu God Shiva and his beloved Shakti. Perhaps because they are deities in the Hindu tradition, not bound by human inhibitions, Shiva and Shakti are able to speak openly to one another about very intimate things—things that we poor mortals find difficult to discuss. Things, in fact, that we may believe we should *not* discuss.

We are a little embarrassed by sex. Some of us are a lot embarrassed. We blush about it. We lower our eyes. Even the vocabulary we have for sex and for our sexual organs is embarrassing—too clinical, too slangy, or too crude. Compare, for example, such eastern designations for the male organ as Jade Stalk and Scepter of Light, to our western monikers "pecker," "prick," and "wang"; compare Precious Gateway, Golden Doorway, and Flower Heart to "hole."

Obviously we cannot communicate without words, particularly in a book. And if the only words we have to communicate with are charged with negative, infantile, or derogatory innuendo, and *what* we have to communicate is a positive, enriching, and laudatory message, it seems we have a problem. We have attempted to solve this problem by adding a few new words to the language of love.

Actually they are old words, Sanskrit words, the same ones Shiva and Shakti used in their "pillow talk." We use the word *lingam* for the male sexual organ; it literally means a wand of light, or God's organ. We use the word *yoni* to describe the female genitalia; it translates literally as "sacred space." Because these are new words to most of us in the West, they don't have a history, and they don't automatically touch off a conditioned response. We haven't heard them used in nasty jokes, for instance, and mother never said, "Girl, don't touch your yoni!" They are softer words, too, on the tongue and to the ear. They need some getting used to, but it doesn't take long. In a very short time, most of the couples who attend our seminars find they are more comfortable using these words than those they may have used in the past. Many couples adopt these new words and take them home; the words become another intimate connection between them, their own private "twilight" language. We hope that you, too, will become familiar with these words as we continue to use them in describing the sexual nature of Tantra.

THE JEWEL IN THE CROWN

The clitoris sits like a bell or a jewel in the topmost part of the yoni. It is the only organ in the body whose sole function is to generate pleasure. Although the tip of the clitoris is tiny in most women, it has a shaft that may extend an inch deep into the crown wall of the yoni. If the mood is right, stimulating the tip and the shaft (which becomes palpably erect when excited) with fingers or mouth or lingam can usually arouse a woman to an orgasm. During intercourse, either the man or the woman herself can stimulate this area while he is inside her. Or one of them can use the lingam as a wand, holding it around the shaft and manipulating it over and around the clitoris, but not penetrating any deeper than one inch. (These techniques are described in detail in Chapter Ten.)

Learning the right touch is important. Overstimulation can short-circuit a woman's building energy. The right touch is something a woman can learn by herself, however, and pass on to her lover, by stroking or pressing or rubbing the jewellike tip and shaft of her own clitoris. Remember that it is not just the clitoris, but the whole first inch of the yoni that is extremely sensitive. Great love and attention are given to this electrical first inch by Tantricas when they perform the rituals known as "Honoring the Yoni," for Tantricas respect the clitoris as the gateway to the chamber that is the source of all life. (See Chapter Nine for a description of the tantric rituals for honoring the yoni and the lingam.)

THE SACRED SPOT

This energetic access spot is the other pole for sexual fulfillment in women. Deep inside, protected as the clitoris is not, it is a place that can produce the most profound pleasure, both physically and on a psychic level. But because it is so deep inside and so well hidden, it is often a receptacle for storing all manner of hurtful things associated with sexuality. If that is the case, the spot's negative charge can be shocking—and it is important to know this when you begin the process of arousing it. If a woman has had painful experiences with sex, physical or emotional, her first contact with the spot may be unpleasant, even painful, in the way a bruise hurts when you put pressure on it. If she perseveres, however, if she and her loved one go slowly and love tenderly, the sore spot inside her will heal, and with it her past wounds; and in healing herself in this way a woman can awaken a power she has never known. This power can illuminate life in all areas, and can provide access to the tantric Wave of Bliss. It is the power of the Goddess Shakti, the power of Tantra, and it can be yours.

HOW TO FIND THE SACRED SPOT

Finding the sacred spot requires a touch that often is difficult for a woman to accomplish alone. She may find a position in which she can just about reach her own sacred spot, but it will be awkward, and she probably won't be able to do much more than locate it, if that. It will be very difficult for her to stimulate or massage it, which one must do to access its healing power and its sexual and spiritual potential. A few women who've attended our seminars tell us they've been able to locate the spot themselves by squatting and pressing up toward the navel with two fingers from inside, while pressing down just above the pubic bone with the other hand. If a woman can manage to stimulate or massage the area the spot will swell, which may make it palpable between the two sets of fingers. For most women, though, this part of their awakening process requires the loving touch of a partner. And he should be prepared to respect the vulnerable nature of the spot, both physically and psychologically. It is most important that couples approach this moment together in harmony. For initiates, both men and women, it's a little scary; it's an intimate connection of a new kind. Use the tools we've described for creating harmony between you and your lover, for example, the nurturing meditation and the breathing and mind-focusing techniques, so that the two of you become physically at ease and in sync with one another.

At this point in our seminars we divide the men and women into separate groups, and in this somewhat safer-feeling environment we talk about the process of finding the sacred spot: where it is located, how to approach it, how it may feel. We use this time, too, to talk about our personal experiences and to share our difficulties and to learn from one another. This separate-by-sex congregation is a kind of tribal gathering of initiates before a ritual. We speak openly. We aren't there to impress one another. The conversation is anything but locker room. Charles leads the men in a discussion of their role in the discovery of the sacred spot. He explains that they will be assuming the role of healer, and that for the moment this will take precedence over their role as lover. He stresses that psychic hurts often reside inside a woman's vagina, and that she may respond emotionally, even violently, when they are awakened and remembered, which may well happen when the spot is touched. As the healing partner in this case, the man must be there for the woman one hundred percent. He must accept her emotions, even her anger, understanding that they are the expressions of ghosts; that the past is spinning out of her; that the room full of her preconceptions is emptying.

Caroline discusses with the women some of the emotions they may expect to feel when the sacred spot is touched for the first time, but she emphasizes that it can be a profound, moving, and intimate experience. She explains that it can be an extraordinary psychological breakthrough for some women, as well as an experience of pure pleasure, a phenomenal new kind of orgasmic ecstasy.

Before beginning, the woman should empty her bladder. The sacred spot lies close to the bladder, and its stimulation may feel at first like the need to urinate. She can lie on her back, with her legs raised so that the back of one or both of her thighs rests against her lover's chest, or with her feet on the mattress while her lover kneels beside her. She can place a pillow under her buttocks for support and comfort. The vagina should be well lubricated.

The first few times you experiment with this, the man should begin by using only one finger to make contact—specifically, the ring finger, which is said to have a harmonic affinity with the second chakra, and which is smaller than the index or middle finger. Slip the finger in gently, and then curl it so the pad of the fingertip touches the ceiling of the yoni. Using the crooked-finger "come here" gesture, slowly pull the finger forward along the ceiling toward the front of the yoni, as if you were returning to the clitoris. Somewhere in this forward stroke—usually about halfway between the back of the pubic bone and the clitoris, in the area of the front wall toward the opening—both lovers will distinguish the spot.

The heart of the sacred spot does not actually lie *on* the wall, but can be felt through it. Its texture is different from the smooth silky tissue around it; it is tougher, and ridged or bumpy, like the areola of the nipple when it is aroused, or the palate of the mouth. The size of the sacred spot varies from a pea to a half dollar, and it swells when it's stimulated, rising slightly in the middle.

The lover's ring finger or the ring and middle fingers provide the easiest and most comfortable access to the sacred spot, with the other fingers resting lightly against the labia minora and the heel of the hand in a position to exert a light pressure against the clitoris, stimulating it slightly. Or the thumb can rest against the clitoris, if the lover is using his index and/or middle finger to touch the sacred spot.

AWAKENING THE SACRED SPOT

As mentioned earlier, the first few times the sacred spot is touched can be a little frightening for some women; some may even experience pain. Many women also feel as if they need to urinate, even though they have just emptied the bladder. This feeling lasts only a short while, however, from ten to forty seconds or so, after which the sensation usually changes to one of powerful sexual pleasure. But this may not happen right away; it can take weeks or even months of healing before this great pleasure is experienced. Sometimes a woman will feel a pleasant sensation the first few times the sacred spot is touched, but it will suddenly disappear; the spot can become too sensitive, so that any pressure at all is too much. The man must maintain close contact with his beloved on a conscious, emotional level, so that he can be immediately responsive to her feelings. He must lighten his touch or withdraw if need be, until she can tolerate more. Each time a couple engages in this very intimate touching, the woman's tolerance will extend and her potential for pleasure will increase. The sacred spot can usually take more intense stimulation for longer periods than the clitoris can. In the beginning, though, the man must be extremely gentle. His goal should be to charge the sacred spot with positive power, to heal any negative residue; his only aim should be to afford her a pleasurable and healing touch. He should not think about orgasm now, but about healing. The woman should try not to think at all; she should concentrate on *feeling,* her mind receptive and quiet. For her this is a sensory rather than a cerebral pursuit.

Once the man has found the spot he should stop, the fingers of one hand quiet in their position inside the yoni, while the other hand exerts light pressure on the clitoris, or rests between the woman's breasts, over the heart chakra, or presses just above the pubic bone, which can cause a pleasurable pressure on the sacred spot from above. In this quiet moment, the lovers should maintain eye contact and breathe together.

After a moment or two the man should gently stroke the sacred spot for about two minutes; then he should stop again and be still. He can apply more stimulation to the clitoris at this point, but he must remember that stimulation of both power poles at once is almost always too much for the beginner. Alternating one with the other, maintaining a balance of stillness with movement, and focusing attention on his partner's pleasure will produce deep sensations. This cycle should be repeated for several rounds. The number of rounds can be gradually increased over time.

The exotic mudras described in Chapter Ten can also be used to great advantage during the massage of the sacred spot. The combination of these elements—concentration, focusing the mind on the partner's pleasure, and balancing stillness with movement—is one way of practicing love as meditation.

The sacred spot may also be accessed anally; with lots of lubrication some women find this most pleasurable. The lover must be sure to use a separate hand or separate finger for this kind of lovemaking, as it is important not to introduce bacteria from the anus into the yoni.

For the woman, the reviving of the sacred spot is an exercise in expanding her feelings. She will be able to tell just how much feeling she is ready to experience or accept, and she will be able to watch that quantity grow as she and her partner continue the technique over a period of months. The man must be careful not to get carried away. Seeing his beloved beginning to respond pleasurably to his arousal, he may go too far, become too yang (too active, or fast, or hard), and may inadvertently short-circuit her growing

energy. During this period of awakening, treat this loveplay as an intimate meditation rather than as an orgasmic opportunity. When the sacred spot has become fully alive its tenderness will turn to passion, and then its potential for pleasure will be easily accessed and easily fulfilled.

NECTAR OF THE GODDESS

When the sacred spot is fully awakened, when it is free of negative influences, then the Goddess and her mortal sisters are able to experience an extraordinary elevation in orgasmic potential, enjoying multiple as well as extended orgasms. Women with this kind of sexual facility may also experience the release of a light liquid, which modern sexologists have likened to a man's ejaculation, and which Tantra calls the *amrita*, or divine nectar. A woman may perceive a kind of joyful explosion of energy when it occurs, but this experience is quite different from male ejaculation. The nectar is produced once the sacred spot has been activated, but it need not rely on stimulation of the spot to occur. In fact, the release may occur to a powerfully orgasmic woman without her even having an orgasm, and it may happen in situations other than sexual ones.

In our seminars we have met women who produce the amrita during episodes of profound laughter. You have heard the expression "losing it," applied to uncontrolled laughter. And you have probably seen someone actually "cry" with laughter. In such situations, the nectar can flow. Aerobic exercise can also produce the kind of energy that triggers the release. The experience is similar to a physical surrender. We say a woman loses control—to laughter, to energy, to love, to joy—when the amrita is released, but really she is becoming one with the laughter, she is *becoming* the energy, the love, the joy. And in this she is *gaining* the essence of these ecstatic feelings, not losing it at all.

Biologically, the fluid appears to originate in one of the Bartholin's glands, which lie on either side of the lower part of the vagina. It is a very light, clear or slightly milky liquid, which can be almost astringent in nature, and evaporates quickly. It may have a very pale flavor, from nearly sweet to slightly bitter, or no taste at all. Since it is expelled from the urethra, the first several drops may have the slightly salty taste of urine.

The amrita is considered highly nutritious, according to tantric texts, and seems to impart its nutrition both physically and psychically. A tiny taste will almost immediately cause a genuine power surge. And both lovers will experience a resonating energy in its presence.

What's most amazing about the amrita is the quantity of it; a woman may produce as much as a cupful at a time, and she may "ejaculate" several times in the course of one loving meditation with her partner. Tantra describes the female power or shakti as limitless; this liquid demonstration of it appears to affirm this. The release of the nectar often produces a dramatic effect. If the woman releases her fluid while her lover is outside of her, it may burst from her in a fine mist, or explode like a fountain, high into the air—up to six feet high! If her lover is inside of her, the nectar will drench his lingam in an incredible energetic bath.

Every woman has the potential for experiencing the outpouring of her amrita, but it is not possible to *try* to experience it or to practice proficiency at it. The only "exercise" that can be used to encourage or activate it, beyond learning to surrender oneself to a deep happiness that may or may not be sexual, is regular loving massage of the sacred spot. Even women for whom the amrita occurs occasionally cannot consciously influence it. When it happens it is a gift, inspirational and divine.

SEVEN

PRESERVING THE YANG ELEMENT

By my inner firmness I have caused my seed to remain stationary in the middle of the Lingam. Thus it is always fruitful, ever ready. This is the power of self-transcendence.

SKANDA PURANDA, quoted in
Sexual Secrets: The Alchemy of Ecstasy

I n our western culture, "sex education" rarely consists of more than general information on how babies are made and very basic instruction on how to protect against disease and unwanted pregnancy. Much of the other knowledge we pick up about sex comes from movies, magazines, friends, parents—and, given the sources, much of it must be considered suspect. Eventually we gain some "hands-on" experience, usually with another fairly uneducated partner. Experienced maybe, if we look only at the total number of sexual encounters, but probably inexperienced and uneducated in sexual intimacy, sexual techniques, and sexual potential.

One of the greatest areas of misinformation concerns the purpose of sex, its goal. Most westerners, especially men, believe that the whole point of sex is ejaculation. Many women also believe this; they may not have an orgasm themselves, but they believe their men should. Besides, a man's ejaculation signals that he's finished; too often a woman prefers that this happen sooner than later.

For Tantricas, on the other hand, the purpose of sex is the conscious creation of harmony and physical well-being, the buildup of sexual energy, and the transcendence to spiritual levels of consciousness. This is not to say that they deprive themselves of ecstasy; quite the contrary. Sexual ecstasy contributes to the preservation and perpetuation of tantric love and partnership; and sexual energy is one of the ways that tantric practitioners achieve spiritual growth.

Tantric lovers experience more exciting, more orgasmic, more sexual loving than other lovers do. There are a couple of reasons for this. One is that part of their ritual for lovemaking, the conscious creation of harmony through meditation and communication on very deep levels, creates an environment in which sex and love thrive. Another reason for the extraordinary sexual stamina of the Tantricas, the frequency of engagement and the depth and length of their enjoyment, is the practice of male ejaculatory control.

Techniques for controlling ejaculation are described in great detail in the tantric texts, but the concept is practically a foreign one in our culture. From the time a boy enters puberty, when his second chakra first begins to release its powerful current of sexual energy, he's pretty much controlled by sex, not the other way around. And in the beginning there doesn't seem to be much reason for concern. A boy in his teens can masturbate like crazy and not experience any problems, no physical problems anyway. Hair doesn't grow on his palms, he isn't depleted of energy, he can do it again in a flash. His semen seems inexhaustible. Of course, if he has been taught that masturbation is a sin, as some boys are, he may suffer psychologically for his pleasure, receiving perhaps his first negatively charged block to sexual expression.

However, as a man ages, his sexual energy appears to diminish somewhat. A twenty-five-year-old male is nowhere near as sexually obsessed as he was at fifteen. By forty, some men begin to experience what they may think are normal signs of aging: It takes longer to get an erection, longer to reach an orgasm; force and volume of the ejaculation are less than they used to be; and after a man has come, the refractory period, before he can ejaculate again, increases. Some middle-aged men require twelve to twenty-four hours before they are able to get an erection again after ejaculating.

The tantric view of these symptoms is that they are not normal signs of age but rather signs of the second chakra's depletion, a result,

Tantricas believe, of the too-frequent expulsion of the life essence contained in a man's semen. Consciously controlling the ejaculation of that essence is the solution to such problems.

Consider this analogy: A boy inherits a trust fund when he's twelve or thirteen. It's quite a tidy sum—to a youngster it seems a fortune—so he's not shy about spending some of it, even lots of it, even frivolously. Nobody talks to him about saving any of it, or investing; or if they do, the advice isn't particularly appreciated. If the boy continues to squander his trust by spending its principal, eventually, by old age, maybe even by middle age, he's likely to find his trust bankrupt. Tantric lovers make a conscious decision to nurture and thereby increase their sexual trust. They invest it in a kind of mutual fund; they accumulate interest on it and redeposit their interest to assure its growth. And this yields them the most valuable kind of wealth—increased sexual energy well into old age.

Because it is such a foreign idea, this aspect of tantric lovemaking encounters considerable skepticism in the West. While westerners easily accept some pretty far-out concepts—mystical sciences and theories, for example, such as astrology or the power of crystals—they are unbelievably resistant to the possibility of sex without ejaculation. The only way we are successful in convincing people about the value of ejaculatory control is by getting them to try it, and in this way gather data about its many benefits firsthand.

But before we get into the benefits, let us say that when we urge ejaculatory *control,* we don't mean to suggest that a man should never have orgasms. Tantric sex distinguishes between the experiences of orgasm and of ejaculation, which is also a fairly revolutionary idea for westerners, who usually think of the two as one. Tantra defines *orgasm* as the internal experience of explosive sexual climax, and *ejaculation* as the external expression of it—the losing of orgasmic energy, in a way, the releasing or letting go of it into the external environment. With extended practice, ejaculatory control allows a man to separate orgasm and ejaculation, allows him to keep his orgasm inside, and enjoy it in its circuit through his body.

He can learn how to direct it and extend it and make it last for many minutes; and in so doing, he can enjoy and assimilate a much higher degree of energy than he would experience from an orgasm that is immediately released. You'll see the difference in just a few loving sessions, using the techniques we'll describe.

Also, when we encourage ejaculatory control, we don't mean that a man should never ejaculate. What we're talking about is control, establishing a *choice* about whether or not to ejaculate. In other words, once a man has control over his ejaculation, he will no longer be led around by his lingam—he will be in charge. This is an empowering realization for a man, with far-reaching influence in all other areas of his life.

We ask now that our male readers think for a minute about how they feel after an orgasm. You're about as relaxed as you ever get, right? You're so relaxed, in fact, that the next step is unconsciousness. Frequently, that's exactly the state a man assumes within minutes after an ejaculation. This is not the same experience a woman has after orgasm—not even if she has released her amrita, the near-equivalent of a man's ejaculation. Women are energized by orgasmic love; men are temporarily wiped out. This has to do with the *kind* of energy each releases in orgasm.

For a woman, the shakti consists of yin, or negatively charged, energy—negative in the polar or magnetic sense. The man's sexual energy is the opposite; it is yang, or positively-charged, energy in the magnetic sense. When a woman discharges her negative energetic field in love, she is lightened by its release and raised up by it. Having changed her balance of energy by releasing a quantity of yin, she is more yang, especially if she has received some of her lover's yang energy, in which case she's positively buzzing. On the other hand, when the man discharges his positive, or yang, energy, he is depleted rather than lightened, left with a deficit of yang, which is the energetic essence of his masculine aspect. Maybe it's just as well that he goes to sleep—he's not really himself in this condition.

80

There are ways of retrieving a good measure of the energy that the ejaculate carries away from a man along with his sperm, and we will describe some of them in Chapter Eight; but for now, let's focus on how to keep and build yang energy by consciously taking control of it. Ejaculatory control is one of the ultimate expressions of conscious loving.

BENEFITS OF EJACULATORY CONTROL

When a man learns the techniques for containing his ejaculate, he is able to make love for extended periods of time—in fact, for as long as he chooses. The benefits that result from this are manifold. Longer periods of lovemaking mean more intimate sexual play, more time for communion through intercourse, more of those electric feelings of arousal and desire and supersensitivity and pleasure. This staying power is particularly meaningful for Tantricas, because the sexual experience is also a spiritual experience.

The longer a man engages in lovemaking, the greater his build-up of sexual energy and the sharper its yang element. This results in far more powerful orgasms than if he had been aroused and making love for only ten minutes or so. And if he chooses to come, having held his ejaculate back for an extended lovemaking session, the release is far more explosive.

Perhaps even more significant than his own orgasmic potential in extended love is the potential it provides the woman, whose energy is usually aroused more slowly. The man who is not rushed in love and who has no personal ejaculatory intention or goal lurking in the shadows of his consciousness during sex, loves, and experiences the act of love, differently.

Frankly, before a man understands and is capable of this control, lovemaking often has more to do with his own perceived physical need for release than it does with love. Ejaculatory control is an important step in elevating sex to the art of love. Don't be surprised if you fall in love with your partner all over again when you use this technique in your lovemaking. Both men and women will see each other differently because they will be experiencing their lovemaking with a different kind of awareness in a different state of consciousness. When a man purposefully doesn't come, for example, the woman understands that he is saying to her, "This lovemaking is only for you. My satisfaction is going to be in assisting your ecstasy, and I want nothing more for myself because your pleasure will touch my heart and my mind and my soul, and *that's* more important to me than ejaculating." The man offers his love-making to his beloved as a gift, and it is received as such. Women are profoundly moved by this gift, and it seems to increase the strength of the relationship, and the power of the love. For many women this experience can be the beginning of the kind of deep psychological healing we discussed earlier—it is the antithesis of a male's taking his pleasure from a woman, using her in a manner of speaking, and giving nothing back. The woman who has been used, bruised, or abused by men will be soothed and reassured by the man who gives to her and asks nothing in return.

In addition, a man who exercises this kind of sexual control often seems to give the woman freedom to finally lose control of herself. Her orgasmic potential increases with this discipline, and it's a wonderful thing for a man to feel he can influence the depth of a woman's orgasm; it does wonders for his own feelings of self-worth. So a more loving, less needy sexuality is fostered, and psychologically both partners get a terrific boost.

Another benefit to ejaculatory control is that the man doesn't feel physically wasted from an ejaculation, so he won't shut down physically, emotionally, and mentally after sex. This, obviously, can be of great importance to the woman who is often frustrated by the sudden withdrawal, literally and figuratively, of her partner, especially if she hasn't had an orgasm herself. Even when both do experience orgasms, his shutting down can be disappointing to the woman, because her orgasm has left her with lots of energy; she wants to talk, cuddle, be intimate—and he's not available emotionally. In fact, he's probably snoring away. But when a man practices

control, he won't be snoring. The refractory period is very short between erections for men who learn to control their ejaculation. Since he hasn't spent his sexual energy, he's able to make love again if he wants to, or if his beloved does. And his unspent yang energy, earning interest from her yin essence, increases. Tantricas have more energy, more vitality for all areas of life when they practice this technique.

We've noticed another benefit for men when they use this kind of control—they look younger. If a man doesn't ejaculate there are no bags under his eyes the next morning, his skin looks smoother, and there's a kind of glow that's noticeably missing when he's over-spent his yang energy. This benefit may not be so obvious in younger men, but for men approaching middle age or older, there's quite a difference.

In all this, it's important to remember that every man operates at a different level of energy; each man has to discover his own formula for how often he chooses to release. Some men can ejaculate three or four or more times a week with no ill effect; others may find themselves feeling a little zombielike if they ejaculate that often. There are just two rules: The first is *never force an ejaculation;* the second is *never stop an ejaculation once it has started.*

Most men have tried to force their ejaculation at one time or another. It happens sometimes with extended sex, sometimes even with masturbation, when for some reason a man can't come, much as he might want to. Instead of accepting this, he tries to force it—rubbing and pulling and manhandling himself until he drives that ejaculate out. This is detrimental to physical well-being, seriously lowers resistance to disease, and reduces vitality.

There can be any number of reasons for a man to experience this kind of unwilling sex. Eastern theorists recognize a cyclical period in men during which the energy of the sex chakra becomes retrograde in a way, and requires recharging. When a man's second chakra is so affected or stressed by external circumstances, he may experience what seems like sexual dysfunction or a lowering of libido. The sensitive sexual center can be affected by emotional or psychological tension, by physical exhaustion or illness, by some medications or drugs, and by the influence of the energy centers on either side of it—the base chakra, whose energy responds to material issues, and the navel chakra, which is tuned to power issues.

Whatever the cause, when a man's sex drive seems to be in first gear he mustn't grind it into third. He should allow the second chakra a period of rest, a little R&R to replenish itself in its natural way. He can still delight his partner, build intimacy, and connect with his heart.

Women should also be sensitive to this rule, and not encourage an ejaculation that isn't forthcoming. Some women have the misguided idea that they're doing their lover a favor by trying to help him ejaculate when he is having difficulty doing so.

It is also important not to interrupt an ejaculation if it has already begun; this can cause a bladder infection, or distress the prostate gland, or both.

There are four levels to ejaculatory control. Once a man recognizes the benefits we've just discussed, and desires to master his ejaculations, he has achieved the first level. Level two consists of learning and practicing specific techniques to accomplish control. Level three is attained when a man has mastered his sexual energy, when he is able to exercise a conscious choice in the matter of his ejaculation. When a man reaches level four he has become adept at manipulating this energy—he has mastered techniques for generating, transmitting, and absorbing chakra energy with the lingam. Let us turn our attention now to level two and the specific techniques that can be practiced to control ejaculation.

TECHNIQUES FOR ACHIEVING EJACULATORY CONTROL

A man needs to become sensitive to his normal sexual response pattern, which usually expresses itself in three or four phases. The first phase is arousal, before he begins to anticipate the orgasm. Phase two is the period when he's aware he's getting close to his orgasm. This period builds quickly once it's felt, mainly because the man usually speeds up at this point. Phase three is orgasm and ejaculation; among advanced Tantricas, phase three is orgasm, phase four is ejaculation. Control techniques are applied during phase one or two; beginners should start during phase one. The goal of the techniques we are going to describe is to prolong phase two and thereby extend the length of lovemaking.

During phases one and two, the arousal period, all the chakras are affected, turned on, and they begin emitting energy that is inexorably drawn down to the high-voltage second chakra. With enough buildup of energy in that center discharge is inevitable, so the tantric way is to reverse the current, consciously and physically, propelling the now sexually charged energy back up to the various chakras. There are three internal practices that help turn the energy away from the second chakra, and three external ones. Let's look at the internal ones first.

Internal Practices

1. *PC Muscle Manipulation*

If you could look up into the body through the pelvic floor, you would see a muscle that acts as a kind of cradle for the sexual organs, the urethra, and the rectum. It's called the *pubococcygeal muscle,* or PC muscle for short, and because of its significant role in sexual enjoyment it is often referred to as the "love muscle." This hammocklike muscle extends from the back and base of the spine, where it's tied off at the coccyx, to the front of the body, where it connects at the pubic bone. It is the major muscle of contraction in the female orgasm; the stronger a woman's PC muscle, the more powerful her orgasms and the more likely the experience of multiple and extended orgasms. The PC muscle is also of great importance in male orgasms. For the man, a strong love muscle makes for a strong, firm erection, increases the power and duration of orgasm, and allows him to separate orgasm from ejaculation.

Both men and women can get a feeling for the location and potential of the love muscle in this way: The next time you urinate, try to stop the flow of urine by clenching. If the PC muscle is weak, an army of nearby muscles, including the abdominal and anal sphincter muscles, will contract along with the PC muscle, but in fact it is the love muscle that tightens around the urethra and shuts off the stream of urine. To help strengthen your love muscle, make it a habit to do this clenching exercise twice every time you urinate. As the PC muscle gains strength, you will be able to distinguish it from the other nearby muscles. (Further discussion of the love muscle, as well as additional strengthening exercises, can be found in Chapter Nine.)

Once a man has developed a strong PC muscle, he has taken a giant step toward ejaculatory control, for as soon as he begins to experience impending orgasmic feelings, he can clench and hold this muscle in a sustained contraction that will reverse the flow of sexual energy away from the second chakra. Try it the next time you and your partner are making love. As the man starts to feel an impending orgasm, both partners should stop all movement, and the man should focus attention on his PC muscle, clenching and holding it. He should remain still and breathe slowly and deeply until the feeling of urgency has passed.

2. Breath Control

Breath control is the second internal method for reversing the flow of sexual energy. Some very practiced yogis can hold back ejaculation by means of breath control alone. Respiration increases as an orgasm becomes imminent, so consciously slowing and deepening the breath can make a big difference. As the man is clenching his PC muscle, both partners should remain very still and connect with each other with their hearts and with their eyes. The woman should match her breathing to her lover's as he slows himself, and she should visualize with him the current of his energy flowing up toward the higher chakras.

3. Shifting Focus to the Higher Chakras

As the two partners connect during this still, quiet moment they are likely to experience a profound feeling of intimacy, and as they begin to focus on the higher chakras, the fourth (heart) and sixth (between the eyebrows), they will also be channeling energy away from the second chakra.

Men should not worry about the diminishing of their erection. This is bound to occur as the yang energy retreats from the lingam; usually a man will lose only about twenty percent, and when the erection returns, having touched base with its original energy source, it will be stronger than before. Men will discover that their level of passion increases, their erections last longer, and the quality of their loving is enriched.

External Practices

1. *The Pull*

To perform this technique, either the man or the woman gently squeezes and pulls down on the scrotum, holding for ten to thirty seconds. Be careful not to squeeze the testicles, but just above them where the sac meets the lingam. This can be a very discreet gesture the man performs himself, or the woman can do it as she caresses the perineal area and scrotum. This technique assures that the man will not ejaculate; at the same time it allows him to stay inside the woman, even with a softer erection.

2. *The Press*

The press is applied to what we call the male sacred spot, which is centered in the perineum, in the area we refer to as "his missing three inches of lingam." We usually consider the lingam to extend from its tip to the place where the shaft joins the testicles, but in fact the lingam continues through the testicles, travels under the skin another three inches, and ends at the anus. During lovemaking, these missing three inches respond just like the rest of the lingam; they swell and become hard and extremely sensitive to stimulation. Westerners are often unaware of the pleasure that can be generated with some attention to this part of a man's body.

The sacred spot is distinguished by a slight indentation on the perineum midway between the testicles and the anus, when the lingam is erect. Pressure applied to this spot will turn around the direction of ejaculatory energy in ten to thirty seconds. Either lover should use the index and middle fingers to apply a gentle but firm touch. This technique allows the man's energy to be rechanneled without requiring that he stop moving, or withdraw from his beloved. As you become proficient at it, especially when you're practiced in allowing your touch to extend energetically beyond the surface of the skin, the amount of pressure required lessens.

3. *The Squeeze*

A squeeze around the frenulum is the third external method to prevent ejaculation. The frenulum, located about an inch down from the tip of the penis, is composed of a kind of epidermal tissue that is similar to the tissue of the mouth's frenulum. (The frenulum of the mouth is a highly charged receptor for sexual energy that stretches, weblike, from the gum just above the two front teeth to the upper lip.) The lingam's frenulum is extremely sensitive and responds within ten to thirty seconds to a firm squeeze, almost as if to a circuit breaker. Although the erection is temporarily wilted and the desire for orgasm calmed, both return within minutes of resuming lovemaking.

We cannot predict how long a man will be able to sustain active intimacy, riding arousal to the edge of orgasm and orgasm to the edge of ejaculation, but we can predict with confidence that he will get better with practice and that by rerouting his sexual energy in this way not only will he extend his lovemaking but also he and his partner will share a much deeper experience than ever before.

EIGHT

THE DANCE OF LOVE

On with the dance! let joy be unconfined.

LORD BYRON, *Childe Harold's Pilgrimage,* canto III, stanza 22

We have already seen that lovemaking in the tantric sense, conscious lovemaking, does not come naturally; it must be learned, and couples must learn it together. They must be teachers, one to the other, and pupils of one another as well. Tantra is most explicit in its instructions for carrying out this education in the art of lovemaking, a multimedia art that combines increased consciousness with the five physical senses of taste, touch, smell, sight, and sound, as well as the more ethereal psychic and spiritual senses, to compose its dance of love.

There is a theory that good sex is spontaneous sex. Remember that conversation regarding spontaneity that led to problems for Linda and Sam? Well, they are not alone. After their initial love affair, many couples go through a period that feels like boredom or tedium. This is a crucial time for lovers. They've established a routine: They get up, go out, come home, have dinner, watch the tube, go to bed, and get up again. Sex enters in somewhere between going to bed and getting up; it becomes part of the routine. And frankly, it's not as much fun.

Proponents of the "spontaneous sex is better sex" school are probably not couples—especially not working couples or couples with kids. For couples, spontaneity is usually exchanged for continuity. Tantricas, who celebrate lovemaking as a ritual, which is about as nonspontaneous as you can get, are not proponents of impulsive sex, but they do practice spontaneity in the *expression* of their love. The dance of love is made up of spontaneous, not choreographed, movement—although many couples do choreograph their lovemaking in a way, remembering and repeating those combinations of movements that provide particular pleasure.

Since the focusing of one's mind on one's partner and the nurturing of the relationship are at the heart of conscious loving, the act of love is performed quite literally with "pre-meditation." Conscious lovers ritualistically designate a time for loving trysts; they prepare themselves mentally for their lovemaking; they prepare a place for it to assure privacy and comfort; and they bathe and prepare their bodies for the delight and delectation of the other.

Mental preparation for love is an important ritual for Tantricas before they begin their sexual sharing. It ensures that the love exchanged will not be tainted with stress from external factors—anxiety brought home from the office, for instance, or residual emotional pain from a child's traumatic first day at school or visit to the dentist. The two lovers turn their minds away from the world's affairs and toward each other. They employ White Tantra, yantras, breathing techniques, visualizations, and the nurturing position's subtle synchronization to achieve a meditative mind. This is conscious preparation for conscious loving.

If being in the right frame of mind sets the mood, so does preparing the right place to be together. Ideally it is a private place, where the couple won't be disturbed by the phone ringing or interrupted by inquisitive children. Many Tantricas make their bedroom a kind of temple, beautifying it with art, crystals, draperies, and spreads, sheets, and pillows of various texture, color, and design. They make it an aromatic place, with fresh flowers or delicate incenses. Over time an aura of harmony is created in this room that seeps into the very furnishings. In order to preserve this atmosphere, the couple always takes their disagreements outside of the bedroom, saving this place exclusively for love.

A ritual bath or cleansing, together or separately, should precede lovemaking. Think of it as more than a service to hygiene. It is a purification, a washing away of the cares of the day and a cleansing of the energetic as well as the physical body in preparation for a spiritual union. Focus your mind on the bath as a rite, and allow it to become part of your loving meditation.

Applying lotions or oils after bathing may also be part of the preparation, but remember that the body's own odors, especially its sexual odors, have aphrodisiac qualities, as does the way the body tastes. Since taste and smell are two of the several aspects of the tantric dance of love, don't mask them. Especially don't use deodorants, which not only taste bad, but repress and restrict the body's natural erotic perfumes.

It's hardly necessary to say that you should look good for your lover. In this dance you will assume the roles of God and Goddess, radiant beings. You *will* be beautiful in each other's eyes. But remember that the energy that goes into attracting your beloved is itself a kind of sexual energy you can bring to one another. So take care of your appearance and your adornments—men should shave if they have a coarse beard; fingernails should be kept trim. This kind of attention is another aspect of conscious loving.

Learning the dance of love is going to sound very simple when we tell you that there are only three steps to it, all of which are familiar. But then we will explain that each of the three steps has numerous variations, and that each variation has two aspects, the receptive yin aspect and the active yang. The yin/yang concept is really the foundation on which the love dance rises to its astonishing heights. You'll see it as the heel-and-toe, the chorus, the repeating refrain in all aspects of the dance. Its proper combination is like spontaneous combustion, a catalyst for ecstasy as well as spiritual fulfillment. Between the yin and yang poles there are seven gradations or levels of expression, from the most gentle to the firmest, from the slowest to the fastest. Multiply all this by two, because there are two dancers alternating as giver and receiver at each turn, and you begin to appreciate that this fandango is a bit more challenging than the Texas two-step.

STEP ONE: KISSES

Kisses can range from a superficial peck on the cheek to a soul-shaking experience. Tantric techniques for these deeper kisses are designed to stir the shakti and at the same time release energy from the crown chakra down through the body. Kissing is especially recommended on all of the seven energy centers, front and back, but couples should kiss any other part of the body as well. Kisses run the seven-level gamut of expression from yin to yang, from soft lips to firmest, from lightest pressure to hardest, from most shallow to deepest. Lips should be soft and pliant and the jaw and facial muscles should be relaxed, to facilitate the exchange of energy and increase sexual pleasure.

There are five basic methods for kissing mouth to mouth, and they apply as well when delivered to any part of the body. *Lipping* is the kissing technique partners use to contact the soft, moist inner (yin) side of each other's upper and lower lips, as well as the dryer, rougher-textured (yang) outside. *Tonguing* uses the tongue to lick the lover's lips, to touch the inner cheek or explore the upper palate, or to caress the other's tongue. *Love bites* are imparted to the inside and outside of the other's upper and lower lips. The bites should be made yin to yang, but yang in this category should register considerably gentler than seven on the tantric seismograph. The *sucking* and *blowing kisses* are a kind of inhalation and exhalation against the other's lips, or chakra areas, or across any expanse of skin.

Kissing is a step in the dance of love that begs the exchange of yin and yang not only by using the seven levels of yin to yang expression, but also by alternating the receiving of kisses with the giving of them. The woman should *take* her lover's mouth using all five techniques: lipping, tonguing, biting, sucking, and blowing, and then she should *give* her mouth to her lover for his pleasure— and hers. The man should *take* the woman's lips in the same way, and then *give* his mouth to her for more delight. Remember that in conscious loving the partners continually change roles as active and receptive lovers, and while there is no design for the exchange, no intermission or musical interlude, no set time designation, it is suggested that partners share these roles equally.

STEP TWO:
THE CONSCIOUS TOUCH

Many cultures recognize the power potential in what is sometimes called the "laying on of hands." In Tantra, touch is one of the primary means of awakening and directing energy, and it is performed in all its variety on a conscious level of heightened awareness that contains several aspects, not the least of which is a sensitivity to the effect of the touch on the loved one.

Another aspect of heightened awareness is the conscious realization that hands don't end at their fingertips, and that their influence does not stop at the skin's surface. Our bodies are containers of great energy—we refer to it collectively as the "life force" or animating current. As long as we are alive we emanate that energy, and it manifests itself in an energetic field or aura surrounding and penetrating the body. Tantricas know that the flow of this energy can be consciously aroused and directed. When directed out of the fingers, or out of the palms of the hands, the energy is long-ranging and penetrable, like a lit candle whose heat exceeds the boundary of wax and wick. If you can imagine, feel, or visualize an energetic glow coming from your hands and fingers when you touch another person, you will connect on a deeper energetic level.

As with kisses, the tantric discipline recognizes a variety of kinds of touches to apply to the joyful dance. The *static touch* is performed by "running energy." Rest both hands upon your lover, and don't move at all. As your hands lie still, consciously direct energy from your right hand into and through your lover, and then consciously accept it back into your left hand. You might consider the static touch as an energetic game of catch. The *moving touch* travels in short or long strokes across the skin or in specific patterns (circles, spirals, triangles, crosses, etc.). *Squeezing* includes a kneading

touch and gentle pinching. *Scratching* with the fingernails or tips of the fingers, like love bites in the category of kisses, is usually preferred more yin than yang. In the *Kama Sutra,* one of the best known tantric texts, the seventh level of yang in both the biting kiss and scratching touch draws blood. We don't recommend you go that far—most couples prefer to stop at around level five.

Tapping or *slapping* can arouse great passion. Obviously some parts of the body are better suited to receive this kind of touch than others, the buttocks in particular, because they are well padded and protected. Be conscious of the line between pleasure and pain and conscious of your beloved's level of tolerance; Tantra does not promote masochism or sadism, and this is a dance, not a fight.

Touching might be called "kissing with the hands," and similar techniques apply to both; touch your lover everywhere, focusing on the front and back of the seven chakra centers. As with kisses, employ the seven levels of speed and pressure, from the most yin, or slowest and lightest, barely brushing the skin, to the most yang, or fastest and strongest. Alternate yin and yang strokes as well as types of touches.

Once again, these various means of touching require the conscious participation of both partners as giver and receiver. This means that each partner recognizes his or her role at the moment and experiences it actively, even if it is a passive role. For instance, when a man bestows a long smooth caress with the palm of his hand over his beloved's back and down to her buttocks, and then squeezes the flesh of her buttocks, and continues down her thighs with the lightest possible brushing of his fingertips, he is conscious of the fact that he is acting on purpose to fire her, to pleasure her— to arouse her passion and her shakti or sexual electricity—with his touch. But no matter how good his technique, or how loving his caress, if she is not consciously receptive, if her mind is a million miles away, nothing will happen. The receiver must be as conscious of the gift offered as the giver is of bestowing it. Ultimately it is the mind that directs the touch, and it is the mind that accepts it.

There is another yin/yang aspect to touching. As you pleasure your partner with your touch, you also receive sensual pleasure from the contact. Consider it the other side of the touch, your lover's skin against your hand, and delight in the feel of it, its texture, its softness or hardness, its warmth and the energy it emits. Your hand, active because it is touching, is also receptive because it feels. Never "take" with your touch; always give and receive. Women are especially sensitive to the difference, and are far less receptive to a taker than to one who will be a receiver of their gifts.

There are three areas of the hand that transmit different qualities of energy and physical sensation to the receiver. For any of the touches, alternate these three parts of your hand as you caress your lover: just the tips of your fingers; the base of your fingers and palm; and the heel of your hand.

STEP THREE: 1001 MOVEMENTS

If touching is the hand's way of loving, and kissing is the mouth's, pelvic movement is the way the lingam and yoni demonstrate love. We call it the 1001 movements, but you're not constrained to a mere 1001; in the tantric texts, 1001 means infinite and innumerable. Nor is this part of the dance "for men only," because while it is his organ that dances, it is her yoni the lingam dances with, and in this aspect of the dance of love, as in all the others, the partners alternate the lead.

Some women may initially feel awkward, embarrassed, or self-conscious about assuming the lead or yang function in performing the various pelvic movements, especially if they are still untangling from propaganda about what a woman's role should be. These women should persevere. Awkwardness dissolves quickly, embarrassment becomes a flush of arousal for women who allow themselves to take their own pleasure in this way, and self-consciousness is the first level of a much higher consciousness.

In the same way, some men may not be terribly comfortable in the receptive or yin role. For a lot of men, taking the lead in lovemaking is a measure of their masculinity, their ego, how yang they are. Super macho types may even feel threatened by a woman who takes the active role in lovemaking. It is important for these men to realize how very limiting it is to be the giver only. It means the man doesn't ever really get to *receive* the woman's love, even though they may have a lot of sex. It means he never knows what a joy it is to lie back and be made love to, to be honored in this way; it means he will never see her find her own pleasure, which can be a wonderful instruction for a man, as well as a highly erotic experience for both partners. When a woman makes love to a man, she not only delights him but also shows him what is most pleasurable to her. How she moves, what kinds of connections she seeks with him, her touch, her speed, the angle of entry she uses to take her lover's lingam into herself are all a kind of nonverbal instruction.

Just as the kisses and touching steps of the dance of love have a variety of yin and yang expressions, so, too, do the 1001 movements. Although the lingam is a yang organ during intercourse, it must manifest both yin and yang energy, just as kissing and touching do; it can express the seven levels through various means. The first level to consider is *depth*. The most yin expression of depth is the shallowest, teasing or rubbing against the beloved's vaginal lips; a little more yang penetrates just a little deeper; and the most yang expression manifests in the deepest contact. Remember that the first inch of the vagina is the most sensitive to contact, and that since the yoni is more yin than yang itself, a woman may prefer a more yin than yang expression of the lingam's love.

Speed is a second type of movement during joined lovemaking, and should be consciously varied from slowest to fastest, just as depth is consciously varied. *Nonmovement* is the most yin level of speed, but even nonmovement can become powerfully yang when the man uses his love muscle while he is inside to pulse, tighten, or flex in *internal movement*. This dynamic kind of still movement is particularly effective in communicating with the woman's sacred spot, especially if the man pulses his love muscle while holding his lingam tight and still against this sensitive spot. A woman can also become expert in love muscle manipulation and internal movement for her own pleasure, as well as for the delight of her partner. She can pretty much drive her man wild with a variety of *bandhas,* or internal contractions. We'll discuss these in more detail in Chapter Nine.

Angle of entry is another consideration in movement that influences pleasure. It allows the lingam to contact places it may never have been before, and the yoni to experience levels of feeling it may never have known. Picture the yoni as a series of clocks one on top of the other. If the penis brushes against the clitoris from twelve o'clock as it enters, and desires to make contact in the area of six o'clock at its deepest position, it would take one angle; if it enters by pushing alongside the clitoris at one o'clock on our figurative timepiece, with the desire of reaching seven o'clock inside, it would take another. And don't neglect the *angle of exit,* which need not be the same. Practice, experiment, discover which angles you and your partner like best. The important thing is to know that they exist.

We also use pelvic-directed *nonlinear movements* ("linear" movement being the old "in and out"). These include circular movements—clockwise and counterclockwise—and side-to-side movements. These variations are very pleasurable for both partners, and they can be particularly good exercises for men practicing ejaculatory control. It's the back-and-forth, in-and-out motion of masturbation and uninspired intercourse that encourages ejaculation.

In addition to these various types of pelvic movements or thrusts, there are several specialized techniques of hand-assisted movements the lingam can perform in loving the yoni. These are described in Chapter Ten.

POSTURES AND POSITIONS

Extraordinary sexual positions and entanglements can be seen frozen on ancient Indian temple walls and depicted in many of the tantric books. These positions were created and performed by tantric holy women trained from childhood in the art of love. For western Tantricas without such a background, these complex postures are difficult and less than comfortable. Better to consider them as emblems of the ecstatic ritual than to attempt to copy them. In our seminars we keep it simple and comfortable by using five basic postures. Each of these postures has hundreds of variations, which can be combined with the techniques for movement we've just discussed to provide a constantly changing choreography for the dance of love.

The five basic positions are: horizontal with the man on top; horizontal with the woman on top; side position with partners facing each other (using either side, or direction); positions with the man behind the woman; and the *Yab Yum* position, unique to tantric lovemaking.

100

In Yab Yum the spine is aligned with gravity, an essential ingredient for drawing energy to the higher chakras and for stimulating the pineal and pituitary glands, which is considered critical for enlightenment to occur. Partners sit erect facing one another, the woman astride the man who is cross-legged and supporting her weight on his thighs. Her legs are open and around him, the soles of her feet touch behind him. This position encourages wonderfully stimulating forms of movement, including rocking, bouncing, and circling; it is also the ideal position for meditating on internal energy and inner life or experience. Note that the slight elevation of the woman sitting astride the man brings the partners' chakras into line with one another, making up for the usual difference in height between men and women. If the woman's weight causes the man's legs to become stiff, or if there is any discomfort at all, she can place a pillow under her buttocks, which will take some of the weight off his thighs.

Comfort of both partners is critical in these various positions. Plenty of pillows can be a great assist in this. Weight bearing is also an important and conscious consideration in lovemaking—we don't want to crush our beloved when we are on top; we want to avoid cramped or tired muscles. Our love dance, therefore, incorporates eight "weight bearers" with which we can shift out of any stressed positions: they are our pairs of hands, elbows and forearms, knees, and feet. Alternating eight muscle groups of these weight bearers in any combination eliminates both crushing and the possibility of cramping in lovemaking. Shifting postures may be done without the lingam leaving the yoni, if the partners move together and the woman pushes or presses into the man to maintain a tight contact with his lingam as they roll over or one moves on top or they otherwise change position.

SOUNDS OF LOVE

In the course of the love dance, couples can add to their communication via kisses and touches and movement, with sighs and cries, whispers and moans, exclamations and other verbal expressions. These are the fifth or throat chakra's translation of the body's physical responses, and they are important music for the dance of love. Since every lover's sounds are different, couples must listen carefully to one another, to the timbre, to the *meaning* of the other's sound. Before they have achieved real harmony or sexual intimacy, many couples are too shy to speak straightforwardly about their preferences; this may be more true of women than of men. A certain kind of shyness makes it uncomfortable for a woman to say, "Listen, I really like to have this first inch of yoni stimulated, especially with these two fingers in this position, and it really feels nice when you touch it in this circular motion, sort of gently, and would you do it slowly, please?" This may be due in part to a woman's literally introverted sexuality, as we've discussed.

Even if the couple is close enough to be able to talk really intimately with one another, the words can sound too clinical or technical. Conscious loving promotes an atmosphere for ecstasy; it's not a science lab. Lovers often find it easier to communicate their sexual preferences by responding to what they like and how fast and how hard with their own sounds of pleasure. They can use this same technique to learn what is most pleasing to their partner. As they listen to one another's sexual communication, their communication in other areas will be strengthened as well because they will be more conscious of each other's expressions in general.

Many people perceive sexual sounds as painful rather than joyful; and indeed there may well be elements of pain in our sexuality on a psychic or psychological level that cause us to cry out as if hurt. Practicing tantric love changes this perception by recognizing the fifth chakra's expression as the sound of ecstatic energy, and by helping overcome the painful and negative program that so many western men and women have inherited about their sexuality. This changed perception is yet another demonstration of the healing therapy the tantric lifestyle encourages.

THE CLIMAX OF THE DANCE

The psychic and spiritual climax of the dance is the orgasm. Most women in our groups agree that the moment of orgasm is a magic moment, a potentially transformational moment. When a woman's shakti explodes in orgasm, she can actually feel the Goddess within her and her lover can feel the God in himself, and they can experience the cosmic connection. This is the ultimate "expansion" of themselves into the beyond.

As the woman's sexual energy builds toward a climax, while she allows her shakti to flow through her, she is in an extraordinarily open state. Remember, it is the yin aspect of a woman to be receptive, inward-directed; so attaining the opposite, the open, expansive range of orgasm, creates a great psychological potential. The woman does not lose her feminine nature in this openness—she is still as receptive as she is giving. At this moment the man can provide his beloved with the kind of healing strength and inner assurance befitting a Goddess. His words and verbal expressions of love will be especially deeply felt.

Men can be similarly touched by words and affirmations of love during orgasm. In this kind of transformational love, or sex magic as Tantra calls it, visualizations as well as affirmations are used in combination with the sexual experience—a much more sophisticated, conscious way of using the mind than fantasy.

This kind of communication is so effective during orgasm because the words go directly to the heart of the person having the orgasm—they aren't processed first by the analytic mind. When the lover tells his beloved of her beauty in this orgasmic state of consciousness, for instance, she doesn't stop and think, "What does he mean? Is it my hair? How do I look?" Instead, in her openness, she simply takes it in, accepts it in herself so that it becomes part of her. She becomes beautiful. When he tells her of her power, her importance to him, her value, when he says that he loves her deeply, these things too move through her, inside her, and become part of her and she part of them; she is empowered by the very words, made important and valuable by them. Words of love and respect spoken to a loved one in his or her ecstasy are among the sweetest of gifts.

AFTER THE DANCE

When both partners have danced to their satisfaction, and especially when the man has ejaculated in the course of their coupling, there is still great energetic potential in the afterglow of lovemaking. This is the time when a man is most empty of his male essence, his yang energy, and therefore he is the most receptive, the most able to absorb energy from outside himself. Tantra requires that the man remain inside his beloved after he has ejaculated, even though he is soft. The energy his lingam is able to absorb in this state, especially if he uses breathing techniques and the more advanced *bandha* techniques described in Chapter Nine to draw energy inward and up, is much more powerful than he can manufacture alone. Couples can exchange this highly charged energy by holding one another and breathing together. They can create a kind of energetic elixir formed of the woman's yin energy and the yang she has received from her lover. As he drinks that elixir in, visualizing its absorption, inhaling its essence, the man receives back much of what he has spent in ejaculation. If he has chosen not to ejaculate, all his yang energy is returned, charged now with the creative and generative power of the woman's shakti; it will renew him, awaken him, heal him.

The time after orgasm is equally important to the woman, not for the restoration of lost energy, because her orgasm is a gift of energy to her, but for the intimate connection it provides with her lover. This is the intimacy a woman wants with all her heart; it is as important a ritual as foreplay, because it keeps passion perking just under the surface, just under her skin. It connects a couple as significantly as sexual union, for intimacy in the luminous atmosphere of after-love, where harmony presides, nourishes all aspects of a relationship, and of our quite human natures.

NINE

SEXUAL SECRETS

All thoughts, all passions, all delights,
Whatever stirs this mortal frame,
All are but ministers of Love,
And feed his sacred flame.

COLERIDGE, *Love*, stanza 1

Before Shiva and Shakti could properly practice love as art, each shared with the other certain secrets. We've discussed many of those secrets in the preceding pages: secrets for creating and maintaining harmony in a relationship, for example, and for healing psychosexual wounds. In this chapter we'll disclose a few more of the secrets Shiva and Shakti shared, sexual secrets that can transport your lovemaking to new realms.

SECRETS OF THE ORAL ARTS:
HONORING THE LINGAM
AND THE YONI

In Chapter Five we talked about some of the negative imprinting that the first and second chakras sustain in the course of our personal evolution, imprinting that affects the way we perceive our own sex and sexuality, and the way we relate to an intimate partner. We also pointed out that early tantric practitioners had a very different view of sexual sharing from the one that most of us have today. Tantra regards the lingam and yoni as gifts of God—the yoni is sometimes referred to as the Pleasure Field of Heaven, or the Gateway to Heaven, while the lingam is known as the Healing Scepter, or Wand of Light. Tantricas experience sexual sharing as one of the greatest of God's blessings, and so they perform certain acts of love as devotions, to honor the beloved through the second chakra. These oral traditions, performed in honor of the yoni and the lingam, are a way of expressing thanks to God, as well as to one's partner. These techniques are considered sacred rites.

For modern couples, learning these oral honoring techniques can restore or reaffirm the sacramental, spiritual aspect of their sexual relationship. The techniques are also tools that can help to heal past wounds to the second chakra, and eliminate negative influences and blocks.

Unfortunately, prejudices against oral sex, based almost exclusively on learned negative perceptions or associations related to our sexual organs, are common in our society. We ask you to consciously put aside whatever prejudices you may have in this area and to consider the oral sexual tradition in its healing capacity. We ask this because we believe that such prejudices may be nothing more than personal hurts in disguise—old conditioning and subconscious imprints resulting from negative experiences that have left scars on the first and second chakras. When these old negative scars are healed, you will find yourself able to enjoy and express a new level of love with your partner.

There are other reasons, too, why some people have difficulty incorporating the oral arts into their lovemaking. We have described how the introverted nature of the yoni can affect a woman's perception of sex. While a man's sex is "up front," so to speak, true to its yang character, outward and expansive, the yoni is the opposite—introverted, hidden. When do women even look at it? Usually only when it's in distress of some kind, rarely when it's in a state of arousal. So it can feel strange to a woman when somebody stares at, kisses, and caresses this part of her body, which she rarely even sees herself. To overcome this, we recommend that women become familiar with this part of the body. Try masturbating in front of a mirror so you can see your yoni when it is swollen and flushed with sexual energy. Ask your physician or someone at your local women's clinic to show you how to use a speculum, an instrument made of clear plastic that allows you to see the rose-colored walls of the vagina and the pearly opalescence of the cervix. Many women are amazed when they see how beautiful this hidden place is; it's a powerful experience that almost immediately dispels a lot of the false and negative information stored in the second chakra. We also encourage men to help their beloved overcome any prejudices in this area by avoiding a goal-oriented approach to loving with the mouth. In other words, the man should not anticipate his beloved's response to the act, or make it his purpose to bring her to climax. Both partners should approach oral loving as a bestowal of a blessing on the receiver, as a particularly empowering kiss, as a healing balm to the second chakra.

Lovers should make frequent visual connections during oral sex. Allow your partner to see the love in your eyes. This is another way to heal negative impressions associated with oral lovemaking. It tells your partner that you find every part of his or her body an object to honor and to love. It is also important for lovers to communicate with sounds as they honor one another. Receivers should use the music of the voice, the fifth chakra, to express pleasure or to indicate a preference. For instance, if you would prefer your lover to be more yang or more yin, you should not hesitate to communicate this. As a general rule, the yoni prefers a softer, slower, more yin than yang touch, the lingam a firmer, faster, more yang than yin treatment. Often we make love the way we would like to be loved, which sometimes results in a man being a little too hard on the yoni, or a woman too gentle with the lingam. Receivers should express preferences, and givers should listen to the sounds of their partner, and watch the body's response to each kiss and touch.

Communicate with all the chakras during your lovemaking. Talk to them; make verbal affirmations of your love and reverence. Sing to them; remember that each chakra has a particular syllable or mantra to which it resonates, and a diaphragmatic humming of that syllable can speak directly to the chakra, especially if the corresponding yantra or image is visualized at the same time. As you honor each chakra in this way, let the mantram in your mouth and on your lips vibrate against the yoni or lingam.

The specific oral techniques used to honor the yoni and the lingam employ the methods of kissing that we've talked about—sucking, light biting, tonguing, and blowing—as well as the techniques of touch—the static and moving touches, stroking, squeezing, scratching, and tapping or slapping. And they should be applied in the same manner, that is, by using the full range of yin or yang expression, always remaining aware of your lover's tolerance.

When you have discovered what manner or combination of touch or kiss on what spot gives your beloved the most pleasure, remember that too much attention to a particular pleasure zone can desensitize the area, or short circuit the energy there. So stay with an area and a technique for seven seconds or so, and then move on to another area or technique. Alternating in this way builds energy; staying constant and steady on one or two extremely pleasurable areas releases the energy in orgasm.

The comfort of both partners is critical, and Tantricas take special care to assure physical comfort during oral lovemaking by "honoring the four directions." This requires the lovers to change their positions in a sort of north, east, south, west pattern, although there are no specific rules regarding which direction to use when. The important thing to remember is that changing directions as well as postures not only provides four times the pleasure, it also assures against a stiff neck, sore jaw, or cramped muscles.

FOR THE MAN:
HONORING THE YONI

1. Remember that the yoni usually prefers a light, or yin, touch, and that for most women the first inch of the yoni (the outer and inner lips and especially the clitoris, head and shaft) is the area of greatest sensitivity and has the greatest potential for pleasure.
2. Kiss the yoni just as you would your beloved's lips, using the same techniques.

3. Move across the lips of the yoni, occasionally contacting the clitoris with a flicking of tongue or fingers.
4. Combine a static or stroking touch to the anus with kisses to the yoni and clitoris.
5. After four to seven minutes of making love with the mouth, spend a similar amount of time honoring the yoni with the lingam. Alternate in such a fashion several times.
6. During her clitoral orgasm contact your beloved's sacred spot with your middle finger, using a static or short stroking touch.

FOR THE WOMAN:
HONORING THE LINGAM

1. Remember that the lingam usually prefers a firm, yang touch.
2. While using any of the kissing techniques on any part of the lingam (being careful, however, not to blow on the urethral opening), contact the man's sacred spot with your middle and index finger, if the touch is external, or the middle finger only for pressure exerted on the sacred spot via the anus.
3. While applying kissing techniques to the head of the lingam, finger the shaft as if it were a flute. This is "Playing the Flute."
4. During your orgasm, hold your lover's lingam in your mouth, pressing its head against your upper palate. (According to the tantric books, a woman's crown chakra releases enormous energy through the roof of her mouth during her orgasm. The lover's lingam acts as a receptor of that energizing essence. In this way she delivers a powerful undiluted jolt of high shakti energy directly to his second chakra.)
5. With a very light touch, using the tips of your fingers, pull and pinch or squeeze the skin of the scrotum; then, with great delicacy, take the scrotum entirely into your mouth, each testicle separately or both together. This technique, which can provide exquisite pleasure for a man, requires the giver to maintain maximum yin—the most gentle contact. The technique is called "Jewel Fondling and Jewel Sucking."

6. The lingam expects a lengthwise stroking that imitates the traditional in-and-out movement of intercourse. For this reason, a stroke that travels around the lingam rather than up and down it, one that simulates the pressure of rings at various points along the shaft, can be very pleasurable for your lover. This technique is called "Ringing."

7. The same techniques of kissing and touching used to honor a hard lingam also apply to a soft one. Letting your lover know that you delight in the yin manifestation of his penis will help him relax and allow him to enjoy new kinds of pleasure. Many men feel that a soft penis is useless in sex. This is not true. We've asked many hundreds of women if a hard penis is of primary importance in lovemaking, and we've never heard one woman respond affirmatively. This is often a major revelation to a man. Many of the men who attend our seminars say that if they're not feeling connected to their sexual energy (if they're not "horny"), they will try to avoid lovemaking lest they "fail" as a lover. What a relief and an empowerment it is for them to learn the ecstatic tantric techniques for giving and receiving pleasure in a yin state. Honoring your lover's "soft-on" can make an enormous psychological impression. It's a kind of acceptance he may never have known.

EYE CONTACT

Closing the eyes during lovemaking is common among westerners, but among Tantricas it is believed to eliminate potential for a much deeper experience, a deeper bonding. Closing the eyes shuts out the lover and creates darkness during a potentially enlightening experience. Conscious lovers should try to maintain contact with each other in as many ways as possible during their lovemaking, and the eyes are perhaps the most important way of doing so; in tantric loving, the eyes are considered a primary organ of intimacy. They are the gateway to the soul, as well as a means of extending and receiving energy, especially from the heart chakra.

Tantra teaches a technique of exhaling while consciously moving the heart's energy out of the right or giving eye into the left or receiving eye of the partner, who accepts that energy and takes it in by inhaling. This is a variation of the reciprocal charging breath discussed in Chapter Three, in which one partner breathes in as the other breathes out. Advanced students of this tantric technique learn to project energy from any of their chakras in this way. For example, by "feeling" his own base chakra, and projecting this energy out of his right eye, a man can "ground" his partner. When a woman concentrates on her second chakra, her gaze can transmit sexual energy. A third-chakra glance can empower the partner. Projecting fourth-chakra energy in this way instills intimacy, and so forth. An important ingredient of conscious loving, as we have said, is to let your beloved see the love in your eyes. Nourish yourself with the sight of your lover.

THE SECRET OF THE LOVE MUSCLE: THE BANDHAS

The *bandhas,* which translate from the Sanskrit as "bind energy," isolate and control muscles associated with the first five chakras, and influence the *prana* or energy of these chakras as well. Tantra teaches a series of bandha exercises that can greatly increase the pleasure of both partners. If practiced for a few minutes each day, the exercises can have profound effects on lovemaking; within several months a woman will be able to play her yoni like a multi-stringed instrument for her own and her lover's delight, and a man's endurance will be improved. The bandhas are also considered a healing art because they awaken dormant neural brain transmitters, which carry messages of pleasure from the vagina to the brain. Advanced students learn to combine bandha exercises with techniques of meditation, visualization, and mudras (hand gestures) for even greater pleasure, but in this book for beginners we will discuss the simpler bandha exercises for controlling and strengthening the PC muscle.

In Chapter Seven, we discussed the importance of the pubo-coccygeal or PC muscle in ejaculatory control. You learned how to locate this muscle by clenching during urination, and how to exercise it each time you urinate. There are several reasons for strengthening this muscle, in addition to increased sexual pleasure. A weak PC muscle may influence chronic tension, which can cause lower back pain. There is also some evidence that an unexercised PC muscle lowers the body's resistance to certain diseases that affect the genital area, such as vaginitis, yeast infections, hormone problems, and even some forms of cancer. The theory is that a well-toned PC muscle improves circulation, which may help to prevent disease by increasing the flow of white blood cells, which defend the body against foreign agents.

And most relevant to our subject, a strong PC muscle (which is known as the love muscle for good reason) allows both partners to enjoy a variety of erotic acts not possible if the PC muscle is in a weakened condition. Women with a weak PC muscle, for example, may have what is called a "collapsed" uterus—although it's not actually collapsed, just not properly supported by the surrounding musculature. This "collapsed" position can make it difficult, if not impossible, to achieve contact with a woman's sacred spot. Toning the muscle often changes the shape of the yoni, pulling the uterus into a superior position and allowing the possibility of access to the sacred spot by the lingam. A woman can test the strength of her PC muscle by inserting two fingers into her yoni and opening the fingers like a pair of scissors. A well-toned love muscle when clenched against the two fingers will exert enough pressure to close them. As we have seen, a strong PC muscle in a man allows him to establish ejaculatory control and improve his sexual endurance. We include two bandha exercises here. Practice each one for three minutes, twice each day, and we think you'll see a significant difference within a month. Men can do these exercises with or without an erection.

The Love Grip: Clench the PC muscle just as you did to shut off the flow of urine. Tighten the muscle, and hold it tight for three seconds. At the very end of the contraction give one quick extra squeeze, then let go. Relax for three seconds and repeat the exercise. Gradually increase the period of the grip to ten seconds before the final squeeze and release. Be sure to relax the muscle completely between contractions, for as long as the contraction was held.

The Pulse: Clench and release the PC muscle in a series of contractions. Be sure to make each clench and each release distinct, completely relaxing the muscle after every release. As you become more proficient you will be able to make the period between clenching and releasing shorter, so the pulse becomes quicker. Count the number of beats between contractions when you first begin to do this exercise, and try to cut that number down with each practice session. Men who perform this exercise with an erection will discover that the rapid contractions cause the lingam to bob up and down; this particular exercise is especially helpful in improving endurance.

For women, these internal exercises are only "tricks" to entertain and pleasure her lover, unless she concentrates on combining the muscular contractions with a focused mind that directs the emotional energy of her love through her second chakra. There's nothing wrong with a few tricks, of course, but these techniques can become powerful tools for transmitting the highest form of energy when combined with conscious loving.

SELF-LOVE IN LOVEMAKING

Masturbation is usually considered a solo activity, but Tantricas find much pleasure in joining that singular delight to the pleasure they enjoy together. A woman can touch herself in a way that pleases her, while the man is making love to her with his lingam. This is a practical as well as an erotic technique; most women know how to provide themselves great enjoyment, and since her touch will also make contact with her lover's lingam, she will be stimulating him as well. Furthermore, most men become highly aroused when a woman touches herself.

KISSES

Remember that kisses, no matter where they are applied, should be made in the same manner as they are bestowed to the mouth. Kisses are especially exciting when applied to the various chakra regions, front and back. Most of us know that the throat and the nape of the neck (fifth chakra region) are erogenous zones, but so are all the other areas fed by the subtle energy centers.

SECRET OF A LONGER, DEEPER, AND "HIGHER" ORGASM

This technique for a more powerful and deeply felt orgasm is based on a specialized form of breath control. As we mentioned in our discussion of breath control in Chapter Two, yogis of all disciplines, not just Tantricas, consider breath control to be of prime importance. It is considered as a kind of life control, because getting control of your breathing can allow you to get control of your life. Yogic breathing relaxes the physical body as well as the subtle body and the mind, and it imparts energy to all three.

To increase the length and power of your orgasm, start to inhale (as slowly as possible) about halfway into the orgasmic peak. The "building up" feeling of climax will continue for as long as you can sustain the inhalation. When you've reached the limit of inhalation, begin to release the breath with as much sound as possible. Really sing out. Don't be afraid of your neighbors hearing you, you may inspire them. More important, the volume of your sound influences the volume—the depth—of your orgasm. But you want to stay in control of the sound and not use it up too fast; the orgasm will last as long as you continue to vocalize it in your exhalation. With practice, both men and women can learn to keep the orgasm going for more than one complete breath, up to four or six, possibly more. The moral of this story is: If you practice breathing exercises to strengthen your lungs and improve lung capacity, you'll have much longer orgasms, because you will be able to make longer inhalations and exhalations.

And there can be even more to these orgasms than extraordinary length. When you open the throat center, the fifth chakra, with sound, you can reverse the direction of your orgasmic energy, which has been mostly south-flowing, toward the second chakra. Opening the fifth chakra is like unveiling a magnet, and in some cases the force of the fifth chakra's "magnet" is powerful enough to pull your orgasmic energy into the sixth chakra, the area of the "third eye," and up even farther, into and out of the seventh or crown chakra. Such explosive occurrences are profoundly moving, both physically and spiritually; they are considered enlightening experiences, and can lead to the ultimate tantric goal of Unity.

Achieving a "mind-blowing" orgasm that awakens and expands consciousness is within the power of all of us. Visualization during orgasm is often very helpful in this regard, and a visualization shared by both partners is twice as helpful: Picture your subtle body's system. Picture the white-gold color of sexual energy. Imagine a current of that energy spiraling through you like electricity, toward your second chakra. As your orgasm begins and you start breathing in, visualize your inhalation pulling that spiraling energy upward. See it move like liquid platinum through your solar plexus, the area of the third chakra, up through the heart center, up again into the throat center and up even farther into the sixth and seventh chakras. Feel the liquid light bathing the sixth chakra between your eyes, feel it enter your brain and, finally, experience its explosion out of the crown chakra. Pause. Hold the vision. You are a radiant being now, with a halo of energy around you.

Now reverse the direction of your breath, exhaling with a great sound to unlock the throat chakra. As the sound of your release floods from your throat, the energy also floods through you, again drenching each chakra as it spirals down the axis of the spine. Visualize yourself as a lightning rod for that spiritual/sexual energy. For the extent of the orgasm you are, in a way, linked to the cosmos.

TEN
EXOTIC SEXUAL TECHNIQUES

If she uses her inner muscles,
gripping your lingam with her yoni's vise,
squeezing and stroking it,
holding it inside her for a hundred heartbeats,
it is known as Samdamsaja (The Tongs)

Kama Sutra

The exotic techniques presented here can be thought of as delectable entrees on a menu of love; each is capable of providing a high level of physical delight for lovers, and each is potentially transformational. Try those that sound interesting. And remember that just as the great classic recipes are modified to suit a particular chef's own preferences, so these sexual delicacies can be adapted to best pleasure you and your partner. Be creative; remember the touches, kisses, movements, and positions you've learned, and apply them with your own variations. Remember, too, to alternate yin and yang in all your loving acts. Don't be afraid of being clumsy; grace is achieved with practice. Focus your mind, and consider your lovemaking as a sacrament in which you and your beloved honor and enrich each other. And now enjoy each other.

THREE EXOTIC KISSES
The Libation or the Nectar of the Three Peaks

Tantra recognizes three parts, or peaks, of the body that release a kind of energetic juice, a nectar, which is extremely nourishing to the receiver and vitalizing to the giver. The first peak is centered in the upper palate and runs along the frenulum into the upper lip.

Stimulation of this peak inspires the release of a sexual dew which spills down through the body from the topmost chakra. This liquid is different from saliva; it's a warmer wetness that suddenly waters the mouth—the "subtler" secretion of the tantric subtle body.

The nipples and breasts with their direct line to the heart chakra are the second peak and source of special nectar. Both lovers consciously give and receive the breast's delicate secretions, which may be a very light milky substance, or a slightly sweet and salty precipitation. Couples alternate as giver and receiver, using all the methods of kissing they have learned, from the gentlest to firmest, kissing the breasts as if they were the lips of the beloved.

The third peak is in the organs of the second chakra, the yoni and the lingam. When we talk about this particular libation we do not mean the man's ejaculate or the woman's amrita, which are forms of a different kind of energy. The nectar of the third peak, like that of the other two, is a juice of the subtle body; it is less substantial than that of the physical body, but its influence in arousing passion is every bit as potent. In a woman these clear rich juices begin to flow with the awakening of her shakti; a man will also release this essential dew when he is in an erect (yang) state. Don't be afraid to swallow the energizing nectars of any of the three peaks; they have been recognized as a kind of lover's healing tonic or potion for thousands of years.

The success of these libation techniques, no matter which peak you imbibe, lies in the concurrence of yin and yang action. As your partner drinks the nectar from your mouth, and bestows kisses on you, you are in the yin or accepting position. But at the same time, as you impart your nectar to your lover, you are also yang. Try to consciously think and feel the yin and yang of the libation. Say to your beloved as you release the nectar of your first peak, "I give these lips to you, I give you the nectar of my mouth." And when you receive the nectar from your beloved, savor it, feel it fill your mouth, inhale its essence, be conscious of accepting it. Think and feel, "I accept this sweetness from you."

120

The Kiss of the Upper Lip

This potent kiss is a tantric technique that uses an energetic conduit between the valley of a woman's upper lip and her clitoris. The lover sucks gently on his beloved's upper lip, using his tongue and lips to draw in on the frenulum which stretches from the inside of the upper lip to the point on the gum directly above the two front teeth. As he sucks her upper lip, she sucks his lower lip and visualizes the subtle channel that runs from the frenulum to her clitoris. Once that channel opens as a conduit for sexual energy, a woman may be able to experience deep clitoral stimulation—even to orgasm—from the kiss alone.

The Tongue to Upper Palate

This is a supremely erotic technique for the transfer of sexual energy. While the woman is having her orgasm she touches her tongue to her upper palate and holds it there for the length of her orgasm. The simultaneous occurrence of the orgasm and contact with the sensitive upper palate releases a deep store of energy from the woman's crown chakra into her tongue. If she then offers her tongue to her lover to suck, he will absorb this powerful energy and its electric charge will pass through him in a direct line to his lingam, or second chakra. Since the lovers are joined together, the energy from this powerful charge transfers from his second chakra to hers, and she may now consciously inhale it, pulling it up through her to be reabsorbed.

JEWEL IN THE CROWN

In any position during intercourse the man can apply light pressure to his beloved's clitoris with one or two fingers, or with any other part of his hand, or a woman can use her own hand to touch herself. The pressure need not be a moving touch; pelvic or other movements during lovemaking will influence the static pressure against the clitoris, or "jewel." Remember not to overstimulate.

DELIGHTING THE ONE
WHO KNEELS ABOVE

To perform this technique of oral sex, the woman kneels above her lover's lips and lowers herself onto his mouth, giving her yoni to his lips and tongue. His role is passive; she uses 1001 gentle or subtle pelvic movements to find her own pleasure. As in all tantric techniques, both partners should be conscious of the yin and yang, the receiving and the giving aspects of their loving.

EXOTIC HAND-ASSISTED TECHNIQUES
Holding the Wand

In this technique, either partner grasps the lingam with the fingers or hand and manipulates it as if it were a wand, rubbing its head over the outside of the yoni, across the perineum to the anus, and especially over and around the clitoris. This is a particularly good method to use if the lingam is not fully erect; the stimulation and contact with the beloved's yoni will usually inspire an erection pretty quickly, but a soft or semisoft lingam can also provide a woman great orgasmic pleasure. Additional lubricant may be necessary in this technique to eliminate friction and enhance enjoyment. Many women find great sexual pleasure in assuming the active role in this technique, leading the dance, as it were, by holding the lingam and moving it to stimulate the yoni.

Tapping

Slapping or tapping the lingam against the yoni's lips, clitoris, perineum, and anus is another hand-assisted technique Tantra specifies. Again, either the man or the woman can perform this move, handling the lingam as if it were a conductor's baton, tapping it to a slow tempo that builds faster and faster, and using it to contact the yoni with a touch that varies from gentle to firm, then back again to gentle. This is a satisfying technique whether the lingam is hard or soft.

Churning Butter

This technique is similar to Holding the Wand, except that here the "wand" is held inside the yoni and either partner directs its movement in a circular motion, varying from shallow to deep, as if churning butter. The hand allows the lingam movement that it is not able to achieve from pelvic thrusting alone. This unique style of movement can be very pleasurable to both partners, and it is a good technique to use when practicing ejaculatory control.

EXOTIC MUDRAS

Mudras are potent hand positions or body postures that profoundly influence the body's energy. The two mudra techniques we describe here are part of a ritual called *nyasa,* an advanced form of tantric touch that charges and awakens the chakras. Nyasa combines mudra's conscious touching, yantra visualization, mantra, and emotion to purify, balance, and elevate the vibrational level of the energy centers. Forms of nyasa are sometimes popularized in the West as *Shaktipat,* wherein a spiritual teacher performs nyasa on the brow chakra of the initiate.

Contacting Three Points of Pleasure

In this combination, the woman takes the superior position, kneeling above her lover with her chest close to his. The lover's lingam penetrates deep inside and makes contact with the woman's sacred spot by its pressure against the upper front wall of the vagina. Now he reaches down and contacts her anus with his index finger. Pressure against or into the anus can provide a pleasurable contact with the sacred spot from a different angle than the lingam. The tip of his middle finger, meanwhile, presses lightly up against the clitoris. Movement should be minimal, as the woman is receiving a simultaneous energetic charge to three erogenous zones; the man must be careful not to overstimulate and thereby short-circuit the buildup of her sexual energy. He should alternate light movement with stillness at each of the three points of pleasure (contacting the anus and the clitoris with a light touch but no movement, while moving his pelvis, for example).

This ritual technique is based on the tantric system that recognizes positively and negatively charged energies (yang and yin energies) at various bodily access points, and seeks to combine them in particular ways. In this case, pleasure is derived from the index finger, which is considered to carry a negative charge, pressing against or entering a positively charged base chakra, combined with the positive charge of the middle finger entering the yoni's yin, or negatively charged, energetic field.

Uniting the Energy Poles

When the lover's index and middle finger contact his beloved's sacred spot, his thumb has access to her clitoris, so he is able to give pleasure to both her sensitive poles. At the same time he can rest his other hand above her pubic bone, applying pressure against the sacred spot from the outside so that it is moved into even closer contact with the fingers inside. Movement should be minimal or static. In a variation of this technique, when the man honors the yoni through oral contact, he can also apply external pressure above the pubic bone.

KNEELING AT THE GATE OF PLEASURE

This technique can be used in lovemaking whenever the man is on top of the woman with his lingam semierect or soft inside her. Without withdrawing, the man lifts his beloved's legs onto his shoulders, and he comes onto his knees. Depending on how soft he is and how big, he inserts one or two fingers into her yoni and contacts her sacred spot, which he stimulates with a gentle stroking massage or pulsing motion. The lingam is still inside, also receiving the stimulating touch of his own two fingers. In this yin, negatively charged state, the man is able to absorb a quantity of his beloved's potent energy.

PRESSING

This is a pelvic-directed movement that can be used when the lingam is erect and deep inside the yoni and the couple has assumed a front-to-front or heart-to-heart posture. In this position the lingam holds still inside the yoni, and the lovers press their pelvises toward one another so that the man's pubic bone and hair provide a stimulating pressure and texture against the woman's clitoris. Instead of the lingam moving in and out, the direction is side to side. Of course, either partner may assume the active role, but this technique is particularly effective with the woman in the lead. Since the lingam is in a deep yang position, a slower, more playful (more yin) movement is recommended.

BASE CHAKRA STIMULATION

A huge amount of prejudice is attached to base chakra or anal loving. Base chakra blocks are often as deep-seated as those associated with the second chakra. But for some couples anal sex can be a source of intense pleasure, and many women find that their sacred spot is more accessible through this kind of sexual contact. Furthermore, a gentle and rhythmic massage to this chakra center, combined with deep breathing and visualization, can have a powerful loosening effect, helpful in awakening vital kundalini energy and in relieving chronic tension, stress, and strain.

Anal sex does require conscious lovers to observe a few more rituals than they otherwise might; in addition to the ritual bath, and towels, pillows, and other items of comfort, fingernails should be trimmed, and the use of a water-soluble lubricant is suggested. Also, to avoid the spread of bacteria, care must be taken to wash the lingam or the finger that has entered the anus before using it to touch the yoni.

Both men and women enjoy this kind of loving. Many couples have reported to us that the gentle massage of the prostate gland, and the area approximately an inch below it, can trigger some extraordinarily powerful orgasms for the man. But if you are new to it, approach base chakra stimulation slowly. Begin with gentle and very shallow digital massage and go further only as your beloved requests it. Communication is important, especially with eye contact. After inserting the finger, pause for fifteen seconds or so before beginning any stimulating movement.

Before attempting a lingam-to-base-chakra connection for the first time, the couple should discuss it. Part of their foreplay should be gentle digital stimulation with plenty of lubrication. Tantra does not recommend that the man mount the woman from behind in this type of loving. Instead, the couple faces one another with the man kneeling in front of his beloved, her legs raised high against his shoulders as he slowly enters her anus. Until the woman is completely comfortable, the man should be nearly motionless in this posture, allowing the woman to perform any of the 1001 pelvic movements that bring her pleasure, along with, or in addition to, the clitoral stimulation she or her lover may provide.

EXOTIC VISUALIZATION TECHNIQUES
The Tower in Rings of Light

This kind of loving, which uses visualization along with a specialized form of tantric massage, requires that the woman have good PC muscle control. Any position with the lingam inside the vagina may be used. The woman visualizes her yoni as a cylinder composed of rings of white-gold light as she performs an intimate massage on her lover's lingam by contracting her PC muscle around it. Tantric doctrine conceives the lingam to be a microcosm of the whole body, just as the science of reflexology conceives the foot. Applying pressure along the various meridians of the lingam therefore affects all parts of a man's body. When her PC muscle is well toned a woman can learn to manipulate it front to back, so that the yoni's gold rings provide an even more pleasurable massage for the man. When a woman becomes adept in this art she can play those rings as if they were separate bars of a musical composition. She can create chords, change keys, compose refrains; and in so doing she can transmit a powerful, intimate symphony to her lover.

During her contractions both partners should envision the white-gold rings of her yoni clasping his lingam, transferring their energetic field directly into the "tower" of his second chakra. In this way the woman's potent sexual juice, or shakti, is imparted energetically, as well as muscularly, to all corresponding parts of her lover's body.

The Tongs, referred to in the *Kama Sutra* as *Samdamsaja,* is a variation on the Tower in Rings of Light. The woman uses PC muscle contractions during intercourse, as if to pull her lover deeper inside her. The contractions are performed as she inhales. At the top of her inhalation she holds the lingam for as long as she can, squeezing it and bathing it in shakti energy. Then she releases her muscular contraction with her exhalation. The man inhales as the woman exhales, visualizing her honeyed energy as he draws it up the path of his spine and into his highest chakras.

Heart-to-Heart Loving

Couples assume the Yab Yum, or seated astride position, for this form of loving, which incorporates the reciprocal charging breath technique, explained in Chapter Three, with visualization. (See Chapter Eight for a description of the Yab Yum position.) The lingam penetrates deep inside the yoni, and the nipples of the partners press firmly together. Now the man breathes out, conscious of the energy emanating from his second chakra, while at the same time visualizing his lingam growing energetically, illuminated, lengthening and thickening. The woman breathes in on his out breath, conscious of receiving his energy and visualizing the great magnet of her heart chakra pulling his lingam up into her heart. She feels her fourth chakra fill with his energetic, illuminated lingam, his powerful yang energy, and because they are connected heart to heart she can, on her out breath, as he breathes in, move that yang

127

power directly into *his* fourth chakra by visualizing her own fourth chakra energy entering him.

Since men are notoriously yin of heart, this gift of the light expansive nature of yang to a man's negative fourth chakra is a great healing balm, especially potent because it is self-generated, coming from his own second chakra but gaining intensity in its traverse through his beloved. Interestingly, women can perform this technique to a great extent alone. In other words, they can do all the breathing and visualization themselves, and in this way they can heal and open a man's heart without his even knowing it. Women who regret that there are so few open-hearted men around can do something about it in this very discreet way.

CIRCLE DANCE FROM THE HIPS

To perform the circle dance, the man lies on his back while his beloved sits astride him, containing his lingam in herself, and moves her pelvis in a full circular motion. Some couples find that a pillow placed under the man's buttocks is helpful in maintaining this position. The woman moves her pelvis at a variety of speeds and achieves a variety of depths by lifting herself slightly or lowering herself over her lover. She can alter the angle of her dance by leaning in or away from him as she moves. While this technique is a wonderful physical sensation for the man, it is the woman's pleasure that is sought; it is the release of her shakti that is the ultimate prize for both. So, as she performs this circular dance over her lover, she should be especially conscious of what feels good to her.

The man is receptive in this posture, but he actively offers his lingam to his beloved. He may press his hands, prayer-fashion, to his own heart, or place his right hand on his beloved's heart and his left hand on her forehead to facilitate the flow of energy and pleasure to her higher chakras. In the course of this dance, both partners should maintain eye contact, and the man should empower his beloved with words of love.

Remember that these exotic techniques are not an end in themselves; they are only vehicles for traveling the tantric path, a path toward Unity. It is a journey of the spirit that Tantra offers, and intimate, passionate, spiritual love is its fuel, its energy. Tantra uses love's energy to spark the light within us so that we may come to know ourselves and one another better. This light of love is a healing tool for lovers; those who walk in its reflection can achieve a radiant partnership, unique and everlasting. We hope the tools we have offered here will light your way.

For more information about
Charles and Caroline Muir's Tantra home study programs
on DVD, VHS, and audio cassettes and
their Hawaiian vacation seminars, contact:
Source School of Tantra
P.O. Box 368
Kahului, HI 96733
Tel: 808 / 572-8364
Fax: 808 / 573-6864
Email: school@sourcetantra.com
Website: www.sourcetantra.com

*The Muirs invite your letters and comments
about how their book has affected your life*

REMEMBRANCES:
PUTTING IT INTO PRACTICE

1. In sexual loving, be oriented toward energy exchange and nurturing rather than toward orgasm or performance goals. Be vulnerable in love, be open; don't try to possess the one you love.

2. Practice a ten-minute "nurturing" or "connecting" love session at least twice a day, in which the goal is not to have an orgasm, but to nurture and exchange love and energy.

3. If you and your partner are too tired or "stuck" to nurture one another, try anyway, because this is when you need it most.

4. Learn to speak to one another consciously, in a no-fault manner.

5. Always remember that *nothing is more important than your love, harmony, and connection as a couple.*

6. Practice your PC muscle exercises daily, both the solo practices and the couple techniques.

7. Men, choose not to ejaculate at least one out of every four times you make love, and remain connected with your beloved after your orgasm.

8. Remember that Tantra is an art form—you'll get better with time and practice.

9. Slow down, enjoy love's dance. Make your sexual loving a meditation, and use the moment of orgasm to affirm and empower one another.

10. Be aware of your hands in love. Make every touch a conscious touch.

11. Keep your eyes open as much as possible to stay in touch with your partner during love in this intimate way.

12. Remember it is blessed to receive as well as to give. Make sure you are doing both; exchange yin and yang roles several times in each lovemaking session.

13. Tantra considers the body to be the temple of the spirit; it is our sacred trust to treat this temple well. Since the tantric partnership is a cooperative venture, we might consider the temple of the couple's spirit as a kind of cooperative housing unit. We are exhorted to care as much for our beloved's body as we do for our own.

14. Remember that the loving techniques used in tantric ritual are vehicles to carry us on a spiritual path to our own particular heavens.

BIBLIOGRAPHY

(Arranged in alphabetical order by title)

The Clouds and the Rain: The Art of Love in China. Beardeley and Fu-Jai. Hammond & Hammond (London). *Great book!*

The Eastern Way of Love: Tantric Sex and Erotic Mysticism. Kamala Devi. Simon & Schuster.

Eight Steps to Health and Peace. R. Hittleman. Bantam Paperback. *White Tantra, yoga philosophy.*

Extended Sexual Orgasm. Allen Brauer. Warner Books.

The G Spot and Other Recent Discoveries About Human Sexuality. Ladas, Whipple, and Perry. Holt, Rinehart & Winston. *Modern research.*

Kama Sutra. Any edition.

Kundalini: The Arousal of the Inner Energy. Ajit Mookerjee. Destiny Books.

New Age Tantra Yoga. Howard John Zitro. World University Press.

Oriental Erotic Art. Phillip Ross. A&W Press.

Sexual Energy Ecstasy. Ramsdale and Dorfman. Peakskill Press. *An excellent book.*

Sexual Secrets. Slinger and Douglas. Destiny Books. *Beautiful art and excerpts from ancient writings.*

Shunga: The Art of Love in Japan. T. and M. Evans. Paddington Press.

Spiritual Sexuality. Charlene Weber. The Christ Foundation. *Course in miracles of sexuality.*

Tantra. Omar V. Garrison. Academy Editions (London).

Tantra: The Yoga of Sex. Omar Garrison. Julian Press.

The Tantric Tradition. Agehananda Bharati. Anchor Books.

The Tantric Way: Art, Science, Ritual. Ajit Mookerjee and Madhu Khanna. New York Graphic Society.

The Tao of Love and Sex: The Ancient Chinese Way to Ecstasy. Jolan Chang. E. P. Dutton. *Good introduction to Taoist loving philosophy.*

Taoist Secrets of Love: Cultivating Male Sexual Energy. Mantak Chia and Michael Winn. Aurora Press.

Yoga and the Jesus Prayer Tradition. T. Matus. Paulist Press. *Catholic mysticism and White Tantra compared.*

Yoga-Kudali Upanishad, Siva Samhita, Gheranda Samhita. Any translation; ancient White Tantra texts.

The Yoga of Light: Hatha Yoga Pradipika. Translated by Hans Rieker. Dawn Horse Press. *White Tantra text.*